Politics,
But Better

Politics,
But Better

An A-Z guide
to creating a more
hopeful future

Tatton Spiller

Elliott&Thompson

First published 2023 by
Elliott and Thompson Limited
2 John Street
London WC1N 2ES
www.eandtbooks.com

ISBN: 978-1-78396-752-0

9 8 7 6 5 4 3 2 1

A catalogue record for this book is available from
the British Library.

Typesetting: Marie Doherty
Printed by CPI Group (UK) Ltd,
Croydon, CR0 4YY

For the whole family

Contents

Introduction

Social Media

Born Free Me

Censorship

Devolution

Elections

Fake News

God

Hope

Contents

Introduction xi

A **Alert! Alert! Alert!** 1
*Why the twenty-four-hour news cycle can
be harmful*

B **Boys Like Me** 9
*The importance of equality, diversity and
representation*

C **Censorship** 17
The problem of no-platforming

D **Desire Paths** 25
Why we need public consultations

E **Elections** 33
Ending negative and combative campaigning

F **Fake News** 41
Navigating false and misleading information

G **God** 49
The role of religion in a multi-faith society

H **Hope** 55
Finding realistic ambitions to keep optimism alive

I   **Interference**   61
Government involvement in private lives

J   **Justification**   69
Explaining policy decisions to the public

K   **Knowledge**   79
*How much do we want our representatives
to know?*

L   **Long-term Problems**   89
*The difficulty of future planning in short-term
governments*

M   **Mental Health**   97
A service in crisis

N   **Nincompoop**   107
Tackling the language of hate

O   **Oceans**   115
How to engage with the younger generations

P   **Policing**   123
Re-establishing trust in a flawed institution

Q   **Quick!**   131
*Preventing the rush to engage with voters
just before election time*

R   **Referendum**   141
Overcoming the divisiveness of public votes

S **Status Quo** 149
Why we need to question the fundamental way we do things

T **Tory Scum** 157
Calming political polarisation and aggression

U **Undone** 165
Why we all deserve a second chance

V **Visions of the Future** 171
Why we need concrete plans from all parties

W **Where's Wally** 179
Do you know who your local representatives are?

X **X Factor** 187
Celebrity-style political leadership

Y **Yardstick** 195
How do we measure a government's record?

Z **Zero Emissions** 205
When problems are too big for politics

Conclusion 213

Acknowledgements 217
About the author 218

Introduction

Dear lovely reader,

I love politics. I think politics is wonderful, honourable and decent. I think that trying to make the world a better place – to improve our lives and those of our fellow humans – is one of the best possible things that we can do with our time.

So much of what we love about our country exists because of politics and politicians. It was a politician who created the NHS. It was politicians who changed the law so that people of the same sex could get married. It was politicians who said we could have two extra hours of drinking time in pubs for the weekend of King Charles III's coronation. All the big things.

It's why I have dedicated my life to politics. It matters. It's important. I've been banging this drum for quite some time. Trying to show the world how good this political adventure can be.

As a teacher, I tried to bring politics into everything I could – running mock elections, assemblies, all that kind of thing. I've made videos (they're really very bad, but they do exist). I pop up on the radio and on TV. I had a kids' show that I toured around the country. I worked on the education team at the Houses of Parliament. At university I ran politics societies.

I have spent years and years of my life trying to talk about politics in a way that is positive and full of hope.

In 2015, I created a project called Simple Politics. It was originally a website before it moved onto social media, and I've now spent the best part of a decade writing, posting and generally talking to hundreds of thousands of people every week.

On Simple Politics, sometimes I like to write letters – a lot like this one, in fact. I always sign off with 'peace and love'. Those things matter. Today, they matter more than ever. In the world of politics, where the stakes couldn't be any higher, where the future of the country hangs in the balance of every decision, where so many conflicting ideas are in play, what could possibly be more important than the starting point of peace and of love?

It's not a message you see anywhere else when people talk about politics. In fact, when I tell people that I love politics, people look at me like I've told them I love olive M&Ms or waiting in A&E. People nod and move on in the hope that the conversation can return to whether or not the odd bit where Eleven finds the other people with powers ruins the whole of *Stranger Things* or just that season.

The problem is that they're right. I'm wrong.

Politics in the UK isn't the glorious bastion of hope that I wish it was. And that I, occasionally, pretend it is. We so often don't take the opportunity to discuss and debate the problems we face in a measured way that might create the better world we dream of.

I speak to people about politics all the time, and what I hear most often is that they don't feel things are working. I get it.

If you follow what's going on closely – as I do – it's easy to get caught in a spiral of despair. Opposition parties who'd rather just stomp their feet than offer alternatives. Strikes in every sector. The never-ending saga of Brexit. The cost of living crisis, or 'cozzie livs' as some people are calling it. The virtually impossible task of remembering who is prime minister this week.

If politics were a couple, it would be in dire need of relationship therapy, while at the same time on Bumble looking for some extra-curricular action. If it were a meal, not only would the food be burned, the whole house would be on fire. If it were a film, it would be a romcom starring any of the six lead actors from *Friends*.

Our politics is broken. Caput. On its knees.

Against that backdrop, people are angry. Extremism is increasing. People don't seem able to talk to each other across the political divides. Even the smallest of issues seems to provoke a furious response – and it's pushing people to desperate measures.

The most severe consequences of this current climate are the murders of two MPs, Jo Cox and Sir David Amess, and the stabbing of another, Stephen Timms. I'm not going to linger on these now (they're discussed later in the book) because while these are awful, tragic and horrific crimes, which must never be forgotten, they are, thankfully, isolated incidents perpetrated by monstrous individuals.

The problems in our system are much more widespread and deeply rooted. A system that puts people off at every stage, that pushes people to more and more extreme positions.

I want to use two snapshots to show you what I mean.

Let's start by taking a look inside the House of Commons chamber itself at midday on 13 July 2022.

Prime Minister's Questions (PMQs) – the most watched event in the parliamentary week – was about to begin. Rather than settling down and getting on with proceedings, two MPs decided to make a scene. Kenny MacAskill and Neale Hanvey of the Scottish party Alba (although they were both elected as SNP candidates) stood up and started shouting at the prime minister, demanding a second independence referendum for Scotland.

It didn't go down well. The Speaker of the House of Commons, Lindsay Hoyle, is usually a calm man. He repeatedly asked them to sit down. They didn't. In the end, Hoyle snapped and shouted, 'Shut up a minute . . . I will not tolerate such behaviour. If you want to go out, go out now, but if you stand up again, I will order you out. Make your mind up. Either shut up or get . . . Shut up a minute. Two at once!'

The two were thrown out of Parliament for the rest of the day.

How could such a scene inspire any confidence in our political process?

No form of government makes everyone happy. There will always be people who can't get what they set out to achieve. That's the reality of politics. What we can hope for is a system where people – especially MPs – are able to communicate in a meaningful way, rather than resort to this counterproductive playground behaviour. Change can happen, but it might not always be immediate. We need to work for it, make our case, persuade people to our point of view. That's how democracy works.

Politics needs to be better than this.

Snapshot two takes us away from Parliament. It takes us onto the streets of Essex. It is 13 October 2021 at around 8.30 a.m. Members of Insulate Britain are blocking a road. They want the government to fund a massive programme of insulating houses, to cut the amount of energy being used to heat homes across the country. They say that it's a reasonable and achievable step to take to tackle the climate emergency. They say that blocking roads is the only way they can get the government's attention and the only way they can get their message across to the wider public.

On this particular day they are blocking a road near the M25. Behind the protest, in the front row of stationary cars is Sherrilyn Speid. She is taking her son to school, but can go no further because of the protest. She is not delighted with the situation. She gets out of the car and shouts at the protesters sitting on the road. She uses language that you probably wouldn't use in front of your older relatives.

She tells them, 'I don't care what the issue is. My son is eleven, he needs to get to school today so move out the way and let me get my son to school.' Nobody moves.

Having not managed to persuade the Insulate Britain activists off the road, she climbs back into her Range Rover and starts to drive her car into the backs of the people in front of her. She doesn't go fast. It's more of a bumping and jerking motion, but it was a deliberate attempt to drive into people she could clearly see were sitting on the road.

Later, she will be prosecuted for dangerous driving, she will plead guilty and receive a one-year ban from driving and she will have to pay £240. She will also tell LBC radio that she felt 'let down' by the 'injustice' of the whole thing.

The driving ban will be a serious issue for Speid. The defence lawyer will challenge it, saying she needs to drive in order to care for her mother, who has multiple sclerosis, to get to work and to drop off her son at school and football.

This is where we are today. Political discourse through the lens of a four-by-four bumper.

On one side, we have a group of people who feel so strongly about something that they're prepared to do whatever it takes to get their message across. Their passion and their commitment is huge.

On the other side, there is someone else with passion and commitment, but she needs to be able to go about her everyday life unimpeded. She runs a counselling service for vulnerable young children, having grown up in care herself, and a podcast about being a working mother. In the trial, she was referred to as an 'inspiring' woman.

As with the MPs shouting in the Commons, there will always be people who disagree. People who can't find common ground. There has to be a better way to disagree than bringing the roads to a total standstill. There has to be a better way to disagree than hitting someone with a car. With no trust that our politicians can solve our problems, people feel forced to these extremes.

And sometimes it's no wonder people feel failed by the system, when they see how some of the people at the centre of it all behave. People who do have influence but choose to use their power for their own advantage.

We're going to talk about gambling. Honestly, it's not my thing, but plenty of people like it. Pitting their wits against The Man. Maybe, hopefully, coming out of the battle with a little more money than they went in with. It can be fun.

But gambling also ruins lives. It can be an addiction that's all-consuming and miserable. There are many stories of people who have died by suicide after running up impossible debts.

Trying to find a way to balance these two things is really hard. Allowing people to continue to bet if they'd like to while protecting those for whom it's problematic is a very fine line.

The government was in the process of setting up a committee to look into how to do this. It's an important, sensitive and nuanced issue. So this is probably a good way for the government to do it, to take enough time to hear from all the experts, to get this right.

So far, so good. But . . . you knew there was a 'but' coming, didn't you?

On 6 April 2023, *The Times* broke a story. They had set up a fake gambling company looking for MPs to help them influence the new policy. They had approached several MPs, but it was only the case of Scott Benton, MP for Blackpool South, that was reported.

There are rules in Parliament. You can't take a big sum of money from someone and then ask a question on their behalf. In the old days (pre-2023), you could be involved in a debate if you declared your interest in it, but you couldn't start the debate or ask the initial question. Now, you can't be involved at all.

There is a threshold, however, of £300, below which you can accept it without declaring it. Which means you can still ask questions and take part in debates on behalf of companies who have given you that little gift.

On camera, Benton appeared to tell the undercover reporters that the way round the £300 figure is simply to say whatever they've been given actually only cost £295.

For example, an FA Cup Final ticket (plus, presumably, drinks and nibbles) could be written down as £295, when it actually cost one heck of a lot more than that. Apparently that works well for the companies and for the MPs.

In the video it looks as if he is telling the fake gambling company that he can get ministers' attention during votes in the House of Commons. It also really looks like he's bang up for using his power to ask direct questions to the government. In short, it looks like he's offering to try to change government policy – in favour of the gambling industry – in return for some lovely sandwiches at Ascot.

This is such a huge issue. So many people's lives and jobs depend on it. How can we possibly have faith in a system that is supposed to protect us when there is such potential for rotten, dirty corruption? People putting themselves and their enjoyment of a bottle of Bollinger over the people they represent.

So. There you go. It's things like this that make us feel like our system isn't working. So, what can we do about it?

There is an old joke. An American tourist wanders into a pub looking for directions. The bartender thinks about it and says, 'Well . . . I wouldn't start from here.'

Honestly, lovely people? I wouldn't start from here.

This is where we are, though, and so this is where we must start.

Over the next twenty-six chapters I'm going to give you some examples that show exactly how and why our system is broken. How it's become dominated by conflict and antagonisation. How we've become polarised, not only into left and right, but also into one camp who are fully engaged and furious, and another who are withdrawn and uninterested. We need to find ways in which we can shrug off this state of affairs and start finding solutions to the problems we face. To keep conversation and debate meaningful when those solutions aren't immediately obvious, or when they are divisive and difficult.

The topics I've chosen to discuss are an eclectic mix. These may not be the biggest problems in UK politics. Some of them definitely aren't. But even those that you might consider to be more incidental still matter. Small changes are needed as much as the larger ones. Every step in the right direction is a good one.

For each one, we'll look at the issues, the problems and challenges that surround them, and consider what we could do to address them. Sometimes it's less a change in policy, more a change in attitude. Sometimes we need to stop trying to improve what we've got and consider a complete overhaul. Sometimes opposing views are too conflicting to ever be truly resolved, but the very least we can do is to really listen to the other side of the argument.

You might read some of these examples and completely disagree with everything I say. Perhaps you'll disagree with all of them. That's OK. That's kind of the point.

This is not something we can fix overnight. Some of the problems we face have no obvious solution. But what's important is that we do something. Otherwise we allow these problems to fester, to embed themselves in our lives, and our situation becomes even more impossible.

We have to dream. We have to act. We have to find a more hopeful future.

We have to make politics better.

Peace and love,
Tatton

Alert! Alert! Alert!

Why the twenty-four-hour news cycle can be harmful

Hoverflies are crafty and deceptive beasts. They fly around all summer long, with their yellow and black markings, lying to us.

'Look at me!' they shout. 'I'm a wasp! Or maybe a bee. Possibly even a hornet. I am really very dangerous. Come near me and I'll sting you. A sting like you've never had in your life. You'll probably die.'

Of course, this is all pretend. These duplicitous creatures have no sting. None whatsoever. The most harm they can do is bump against your arm in a grumpy manner.

The worst thing about this deceitful and dishonest pretence is that it works. Us humans, supposedly an advanced race, run screaming. You should see the scenes that can be created in a primary-school playground.

We don't like yellow-and-black insects. We rarely stop long enough to look at the insect in question and make sure it is indeed one of the stingy ones before we dissolve into panic. It's human nature.

That yellow-and-black combination has crept into all sorts of warning signs in our lives: flammable materials, electrical hazards – and breaking news banners. Someone at Sky News has learned the hoverfly's trick.

In the past most people consumed their news at precise times during the day: the newspaper in the morning, on the TV in their choice of evening slots or on a radio broadcast. And that would be that until the next day. Now? We have rolling news channels, the internet, apps on our phones, chat radio – the constant thud of news, news, news. They have ways to keep our attention. And they're not afraid to use them.

Whenever anything happens – a politician says something controversial, a celebrity breaks up with someone, a crime is committed – it's time to go full hoverfly.

It's time for Breaking News.

Someone somewhere presses a button and the banner flashes up, creating a physical reaction in the viewers, demanding their full attention. Turn the volume up. Wave vaguely at the people around them to be quiet.

The banner at the bottom of the screen soon tells you what you – ahem – 'need' to know. You can exhale. This one wasn't a terrorist attack or the announcement of a general election or yet another prime minister resigning.

It does the channel good, though, to have you gripped. If watching is an adrenaline-fuelled roller coaster, that's better than a calm, gentle and informative programme. We like that.

All of which encourages the news channels to throw out an increasing number of Breaking News alerts. They do it before an event even happens. The Budget is in the diary for months in advance, but come Budget Day you'll get that black-and-yellow banner telling you it's Budget Day. There is no way that this is 'breaking'.

The worst example of intentionally keeping people on edge with no substance at all is on Sky Sports News (admittedly a sports rolling news channel, but it's along the same lines). During the football transfer window (the set times that players can be bought or sold by Premier League clubs) the channel now has a countdown, displayed in big, black, bold writing, that runs until the window closes.

It informs you how many days are left. Standard. It also shows the hours. With over a week left, telling us we have 10 days and 6 hours to go feels a bit specific, but fine. Did I mention they also count the minutes? 10 days, 6 hours and 28 minutes. Also, the seconds. 10 days, 6 hours, 28 minutes and 45 seconds. Also the milliseconds, frantic little numbers that never, ever stop. Unending in their message that this is very urgent and we all need to be in full fight or flight mode. I like football, but even I think it's exhausting.

And that's a fairly benign example compared with the constant barrage of stories designed to keep our attention. The news channels know what you want. They know the stories that draw you in. In Shakespeare's *Troilus and Cressida*, Thersites watches the action of the play and fumes, 'Lechery, lechery; still wars and lechery; nothing else holds fashion.' That was true then and it's still true now.

What we respond to are stories of conflict and scandal. We want to know that an MP has been caught watching porn in the House of Commons. We want to know if someone was partying when we were in lockdown. We want to know about the wars going on in any given political party.

Those banners about the Budget coming up or PMQs about to start are there with a promise of conflict. Drawing you in to watch the circus.

What doesn't hold fashion is the stuff that matters. The debates in the House of Commons in which changes are made to bills that will shape areas of your life. The committee hearings where MPs work together to make crucial recommendations on their specialist subjects.

We are given a false idea of our politicians and our political processes. We see them at their worst, which is shoved under our noses, but very rarely at their best.

There is, of course, a clear solution to these channels blasting their anxiety-fuelling faux news at you. The solution is not to watch them. There is plenty on TV to divert your interest. Amazon Prime has an entire channel that is just *Homes Under the Hammer*. All day, every day.

These doom-laden messages are no longer just on your TV, though. They're in your pocket too.

Just under a quarter of the phone-owning population of the UK has the BBC News app installed. That's 12 million people. Sky, the second biggest (discounting BBC Sport), has 3 million people enthralled with its app. Both apps throw out notifications. That should be a really useful feature. It should tell us when there is something big going on. Something worth knowing about.

You know where this is going. They don't ping us a notification only when there is something important. They bombard us around the clock. One week at SP we counted. Between the BBC and Sky, there were 122 notifications in seven days. They broke such heavy-hitting stories as Ken Bruce leaving Radio 2 and Madonna announcing a new tour.

When we see that notification on our phone, it's not like the banner flashing up on the TV screen. We have to open the app to see what's going on. In the time it takes us to do so we don't know if war has broken out. We don't know if there is a mutant ninja variant of Covid. We don't know if Dua Lipa has tried a new lip gloss.

Even if the alert does indicate what sort of news update we're looking at, it's deliberately worded to trick us into thinking it's a bigger story than it is.

All these alerts keep us in a constant state of tension. They cause anxiety, these 122 little earthquakes a week. It's not healthy. It's not helpful. We need to know if there is a swarm of hornets. We don't need to know about the hoverfly.

The impact it has on our view of politics and our political institutions is also unhealthy and unhelpful. We withdraw. We say they're all the same. We stop paying attention.

We can't expect the channels and the apps and the stinging insects to help us deal with this. They've shown us again and again they won't do that. So, we need to act ourselves. To wean ourselves away from the cycle. To move on from the dopamine hit of the notification. We need to find alternative ways to find out news. A way that's serious when it needs to be, but also doesn't try to be alarmist. To drag our attention away from the titillating scandals and focus on the important updates from Westminster.

This is the aim for Simple Politics. We're on social media trying to be the solution. Posting everything we think you need to know about politics. People do tell me that we've helped their mental health. They say they've deleted the news apps and rely on our calmer and more reflective approach. One person even told me over lockdown that their GP had suggested they follow us.

I won't bang on about that now, though, because I don't want to blow my own trumpet quite so early in the book. Also, I'm aware that we only cover politics and some people do want to read about crime stories in the news as well. Perhaps you want to read a little about celebrities, too. That's fine.

The good news is that there are news outlets that don't engage with these practices. Short-form, easily accessible news. Radio 1 (and all its sister stations) has *Newsbeat*. It's a delightful, informative and mercifully brief outlet. I have met people who avoid everything but *Newsround* on CBBC. These are both aimed at young people, though, so the stories they tell are focused on a young demographic. They're not for everyone.

I've offered you a few potential ways to escape this weaponised anxiety. Take charge of your own media consumption. Start following SP (sorry, I know, shameless). Watch and listen to children's/young people's news. That's not a brilliant selection of solutions.

As a country, we need to do better. We need to find a way to get calm, clear and concise news on mainstream, adult TV (as in BBC One, not Babestation). We have such a wide media landscape. Why can't our publicly funded broadcaster manage to give us our news in a manageable way?

Sky has regular features on mental health, but doesn't look at its own impact. It shouldn't be unreasonable to expect something better from the media. If we need to adjust, surely they do too. It's through these mainstream news outlets that the vast majority of us engage with the way our country is being run. And yet we're overwhelmed with distraction and hype, with wars and lechery.

Perhaps it's just a case of putting our purchasing-power shoulder to the wheel. If we can demonstrate that we won't be seduced by their overhyped hoverfly-esque stories, surely the market will give us what we do want?

We won't know unless we try.

Boys Like Me

The importance of equality, diversity and representation

You probably don't know what I look like. You're building a mental image from these words, which I assume have vaguely posh-white-boy vibes – the floppy hair probably oozes from the page.

I really am that stereotype. A tall, posh, white man in my forties. I can dress quite smartly. I'm relatively good at communication (you're reading this, so I hope you agree). I can talk in public. My work is in and around politics. And whenever I meet someone and they find this out, there is one question I am always asked. Every time.

'Oh, that's fascinating,' they say. 'And, tell me, have you ever thought of running for office yourself?'

The answer is always no. I have no desire to go down that route. I have never expressed a desire to do so.

So . . . why do I get asked so often? I think the answer is simple. I look and sound like someone who people imagine could be an MP. Through the accident of birth people think that boys like me could – and possibly should – be voted into office.

Sure, you've got Rishi Sunak, Liz Truss and Theresa May, but they don't draw as much attention as Boris Johnson. David Cameron was prime minister for six years – an impossibly long time in today's climate. Before that? Gordon Brown. Tony Blair. We don't always have a deputy prime minister but the last ones we had were Nick Clegg and Dominic Raab.

Meanwhile, the proportion of women in the House of Commons is roughly 35 per cent. After the 2019 General Election there were sixty-five MPs from an ethnic minority. That's 10 per cent. A record number, admittedly, but the 2021 census says that 18 per cent of the UK population is from an ethnic minority.

There is a class element, too. Of course there is, it's the UK.

It's very hard to measure class. The line between working class and middle class is less tangible than ever before. One way, though, is to look at schools. Johnson and Cameron were at Eton at the same time. Rishi Sunak went to Winchester, another private school. Liz Truss went to a comprehensive school, but when she was running for leader of the Conservative Party she told everyone repeatedly that it had been terrible.

Sunak, Truss, Johnson, May, Cameron and Blair all studied at Oxford. Every one of them. The only diversity here is whether they went to Lincoln College or Balliol. Only 7 per cent of the country attend private school, and yet after the 2019 General Election 29 per cent of MPs had been educated in the independent sector. Nearly 2 per cent of them went to just one school. (Yep, Eton.)

What have we learned here? We've learned that we don't have representative numbers of women. We don't have representative numbers of BAME people. We don't have representative numbers of people who went to regular schools. Posh. White. Men. Everywhere.

Does it matter? The question about the importance of representation is a standard A-level essay topic. Do we need to have a House of Commons that's entirely and absolutely reflective of the population it represents? Might it be possible for people to make decisions for other people without having shared their real-life experience?

It's possible to make the case that it doesn't affect the running of the country. Maybe the boys like me can be intelligent and open enough to make good decisions. Maybe. (Probably not me. I'd be too easily distracted by the darts or something.)

I've taught in some very multicultural schools. One was

less than a mile from the Houses of Parliament. What message does it send to my then students that they walk the streets so close to the halls of power, but have little possibility of ever entering them? If there is nobody showing them that they belong, if there is nobody making them feel heard, if they never see a reflection of themselves and their experiences . . . then we've lost them.

If we're losing people, if people have the idea that this isn't for them, then they start to feel disenfranchised, as if they're not really a part of our democracy. We end up with a form of elitism – although the idea that boys like me are 'elite' is laughable. It's at best a mediocracy.

Let's imagine for a second that you agree with me. That you're nodding your head as you read this. What we'd like to see – you and me – is a House of Commons where people are better represented. Not necessarily exactly 50/50 men and women or 18 per cent ethnic minority or 93 per cent regular school, but at least a bit closer than what we have now.

Getting from here to there is difficult. We've been trying to address the problem for a while now. At its 1993 Annual Conference, Labour agreed to introduce women-only shortlists from whom the local party members could select their candidate for MP. Roughly half the seats deemed suitably winnable were designated as women only.

That didn't go down brilliantly well. Members weren't happy that their choice of candidate was restricted. Two male would-be candidates took Labour to court on equal-opportunities grounds. The Conservative Party called it 'political correctness run wild' (although they did say they were trying to persuade more women to stand – Theresa May was elected in 1997). Even Tony Blair described the proposal as 'not ideal' in 1995.

And yet thirty-five out of thirty-eight all-women short-lists went on to win their seats in the 1997 election. (The term 'Blair's Babes' was used.) Overall there were 120 women MPs – twice the number from the 1992 election. OK, that doesn't sound amazing today, but it was progress. And it showed that taking action to nudge change into being does work. (There are no BAME-only shortlists. Political correct-ness has never run wild enough for that.)

While the women-only shortlists do still exist, as time went on they have been used less and less – although it is interesting to note that David Cameron was a fan and some were used in the 2015 General Election. Nobody used the term 'Cameron's Crumpets'.

In 2017 a new campaign called 'Ask her to stand' was launched. It now has a national day – 21 November – on which women are encouraged to enter politics. It's designed to empower women, to be explicit about how amazing they are and how much better the country would be if they were more involved in running it.

I've never been comfortable with 'Ask her to stand' day. It feels so obvious to me that women are strong and cap-able and brilliant. How can it be necessary to give them an annual prod? Then I look at the cabinet make-up of any government. I see the sheer misogyny in debates on Twitter . . . Suddenly it makes more sense.

We're still a long way off equal representation. Part of the problem is cultural. As I said earlier, lots of people have a picture in their mind of what an MP looks like, an image that has built up over generations. On two occasions I have lived in areas that voted against the Conservative candidate. Both losing candidates were white and privately educated. After their defeat they both moved constituencies – and got elected elsewhere. They have both held government positions. They looked like MPs. They became MPs.

The solutions we've tried so far have had some success, but there is huge opposition to all-women shortlists and quotas for BAME people or anyone else. And that is very problematic, because when this sort of image of our leaders is so ingrained in society it will never change without a concerted effort.

So, we need initiatives to put things in motion, but what more can we do to make things better without facing a backlash?

It's very rare when talking about politics, but it's possible that one solution comes from across the Atlantic in America, and from outside the world of politics.

The NFL (the Premier League of American Football) had an issue with representation. Nearly 70 per cent of NFL players are African American, but the number of African

American coaches was low. African American managers were also given less time and were fired more quickly than their white counterparts.

To address this imbalance, in 2003 the Rooney Rule was brought in, which held that at least one candidate in each selection process/interview must be from a minority background. It didn't force any quotas. Nobody was discriminated against, like the men who took Blair's Labour to court over shortlists. But once the rule was brought in, just the act of having minority candidates in the process led to them being more successful.

Could we have some kind of Rooney Rule for our parliamentary candidates? Could we have at least one slot for a woman and maybe one slot for a BAME person? Nobody being forced out. Nobody being discriminated against. Just getting people into the room. To remind voters that other options are available.

It's not a perfect solution. Party rules are very complicated and any suggestion of special preference could be criticised as 'wokeness', as it would be called today. And making sure a wider variety of candidates is part of the process might not be enough – there is still the cultural issue of the image many people have of an MP.

Maybe that's changing. Maybe. In 2022 we had three prime ministers, and only one was a white man. Indeed, only one of the last four prime ministers has been a white man. The Liberal Democrats, the SNP, the DUP, Plaid Cymru and the Green Party have all had or still have (white) female leaders.

Once a traditional view has been challenged and shaken enough, a new trend can take off on its own. Maybe the culture will continue to change. The more it does, the more people can see themselves in those positions and the more it will continue. I hope so.

But at the stage we're currently at, it feels as if we still need some small external nudges. Otherwise you'll be stuck with someone like me (but not me, obvs) for quite some time yet.

Censorship

The problem of no-platforming

Life moves pretty fast. One minute it's all *Squid Game* and baked feta, the next it's suddenly air fryers and *Love Island*. My children have just got into Pokemon, so maybe that's sprung back into fashion. Or maybe they're just not very cool.

In this lightning-quick world, you may have forgotten about Amber Rudd. She used to be a pretty big thing. She was the Home Secretary under Theresa May.

She resigned in 2018 after mass outrage at her role in the Windrush scandal. People who had been encouraged to come from places like the Caribbean to help rebuild the country after the Second World War were now being treated as illegal immigrants because they hadn't been given legal documents to prove their right to remain at the time. Some had their benefits cut or were denied access to the NHS; others were put in detention centres and deported.

Two years later, Rudd travelled to Oxford for an 'In Conversation' event to mark International Women's Day 2020, drawing on her experience as a woman in Parliament and also her role as Minister for Women and Equalities. She was in the city, all ready for the event to start at 7.30 p.m. At 6.30 p.m it was cancelled by UNWomen Oxford.

On their Facebook page, they published a post that read: 'Following a majority vote in committee, tonight's event with speaker Amber Rudd has been cancelled. We are deeply sorry for all and any hurt caused to our members and other wom*n and non-binary people in Oxford over this event.'

Amber Rudd had been no-platformed.

It all kicked off after that. Oxford University issued a statement making it clear it didn't approve and promising to take the 'necessary steps to ensure that this cannot be repeated'.

Rudd herself tweeted that it was 'badly judged and rude' and that the students should 'stop hiding and start engaging'. MPs from a variety of parties tweeted their disappointment, including Labour's Tom Watson who said, 'If you're trying to silence Amber Rudd you really are being anti-democratic.'

Rudd's daughter, Florence Gill, went further, 'I don't care if you disagree with her. It's fucking rude. This is NOT how women should treat each other.'

In this book, there are several problems that feel impossible to solve, and this is one of them. The trouble is there is no middle ground here. You either believe that no-platforming is justified – like those students at UNWomen Oxford – or that it isn't – like the University of Oxford. There is no half-platforming in which people can speak, but every other word is beeped out.

No-platforming isn't a new thing. The term was first used in the 1970s as a way of keeping the National Front from making their racist arguments – although denying your political opponents the right to speak goes back a lot longer than that. Richard II did a pretty good job of no-platforming Wat Tyler on the poll-tax issue when Tyler led the Peasants' Revolt in 1381. Chopping his head off was really quite effective.

In modern times the issue raises interesting debates around free speech and hate speech – is a person being denied a platform to prevent them from expressing extreme views, or because they have simply become an unpopular figure? The Windrush scandal was awful. The deportation of innocent British people should never, ever have happened. That said, it's hard to argue that Amber Rudd is someone who uses hate speech and deserves to be shut down.

The UN describes hate speech as 'any kind of

communication in speech, writing or behaviour, that attacks or uses pejorative or discriminatory language with reference to a person or a group on the basis of who they are, in other words, based on their religion, ethnicity, nationality, race, colour, descent, gender or other identity factor'.

Nobody wants to allow people to peddle hatred. It is generally agreed that we shouldn't ever give people who spew hate speech a platform from which to do so.

Far-right views do continue to be a problem. In Oldham in 2001 the General Election took place against a background of race riots. The far-right BNP fielded thirty-three candidates and got more than 5 per cent of votes in five constituencies.

In the seat of Oldham West and Royton, where BNP leader Nick Griffin was standing, it was decided that no candidates would be allowed to speak at the election count. Griffin stood on the stage that night with a gag over his mouth and the words 'Gagged for telling the truth' on his T-shirt.

Decades have passed since then, but we still see the compelling narrative of imagined censorship: people or groups claiming exactly what Griffin did – that the powers-that-be are silencing them, that their free speech is under attack. We see this same line repeated constantly when people are removed from Twitter.

When President Donald Trump was banned from the site he said, 'We will not be SILENCED! Twitter is not about

FREE SPEECH. They are all about promoting a Radical Left platform where some of the most vicious people in the world are allowed to speak freely.'

But the line between hate speech and free speech isn't always that cut and dried. One person's free speech can be seen by someone else as hate speech. Some comments on race are clearly racist and aggressive. Some comments are reasonable and fair. In the middle there is a lot of grey area.

Working out what counts as hate and what doesn't is an almost impossible task that so often simply comes down to individual perspective. People will never agree, and if people don't agree, who can make that call? Once we get outside the realms of clear 'attacks' or 'pejorative or discriminatory language' how can we tell who might and might not be allowed a platform? When are we preventing hate speech that could lead to genuine offence and harm, and when are we simply silencing a point of view we don't agree with?

The debate around immigration, for example, is often extremely toxic. Arguments against migration can stray into xenophobia and even racism. It doesn't mean that everyone who wants to prevent migration to the UK has those views, though. It doesn't mean that those who agree with a policy of processing migrants in Rwanda have those views. We can't just lump them all in together and dismiss alternative perspectives. Sometimes fair speech is fair debate.

The Conservative Party is very clear on this – it wants everyone to be able to speak and to encourage debate.

Indeed, in May 2022 it created a new bill to ensure that there is 'freedom of speech and academic freedom in higher education institutions and in students' unions'.

Conservatives think that ideas should be discussed and challenged. They believe that not allowing some views to be expressed is an unhealthy part of democracy. It's not just Conservatives, either. I've already quoted Tom Watson making that exact point – it's undemocratic.

The new bill will forbid students' unions from denying the use of their space on the grounds of someone's ideals, beliefs or views. If someone wants to talk about their belief in Zionism, for example, they must be allowed to. It's designed to allow different societies within the university to put on events that the union itself disagrees with. Rules about hate speech will still stand, though, so extreme organisations won't be able to use the platform to incite their bigotry.

Universities and members of students' unions are not a homogenous body – among the members there will be a huge diversity of opinion. The bill ensures that all those people can have their views represented in union spaces.

And yet . . . forcing people to hold events they don't want to . . . The Amber Rudd talk was cancelled because the group that was due to host her had a vote and the majority voted to cancel. Nobody should be forced to have speakers on their platform. Amber Rudd didn't have the right to appear on that stage. It seems both strange and regrettable that the decision to no-platform her was taken at such short notice. If they don't want someone, they don't have to ask them.

The difficulty in saying what's hate speech and what's free speech is perennial, but this new bill interferes with the right of people to decide for themselves where that line falls.

Perhaps a better solution might be to require clarity from different organisations – all organisations – to say where they draw the line. Who might GB News not particularly want on their channel? Who might Instagram not allow?

If we could have a level of specificity and clarity from organisations, we'd know where they stood and we'd understand where they'd draw the line. Debates could be framed in the knowledge of the organisation's restrictions. We'd have a level of transparency and consistency that simply doesn't exist at the moment.

It's not about forcing events on people, it's about encouraging events with as much debate as possible. An event without dissenting voices – or with very limited dissent – is a rally, not a debate.

Rallies are fine things. Playing to the home team in order to get everyone fired up, involved and engaged. They're an essential part in campaigning and community-building. But there does need to be space for debate, too. Debate is where your ideas are tested. You hear other people's thought-out opinions. You can challenge those opinions. You can make your argument – crucially, you can win the argument. People are, on the whole, reasonable. They can listen and understand. You can't persuade someone without engaging with them.

Once we've got that understanding of the breadth of views that will be allowed in a certain space, it is clearer what's going on. Is this a rallying organisation or is it one that encourages a real debate?

If there had been that clarity at this International Women's Day event in Oxford in 2020, the mess about cancelling at such short notice wouldn't – couldn't – have happened.

Desire Paths

Why we need public consultations

Pavements are the best. Firm and even. They keep you off the road. They keep you out of the bushes. Onwards they stretch, as far as the eye and the legs can go.

Sure, they're not perfect. They're used by cyclists when they shouldn't be. Not all dog owners clear up after their charges. There are those three-barrel drain covers that someone once told me were bad luck to stand on and I still go to enormous lengths to avoid.

But the problem with a pavement is that they don't always go the way you want them to go. They go round things. They take the long way.

There are lots of possible reasons for this. It might be that the planner looked at the lie of the land and decided it was safer. It might be a pavement on a historic path-way that's always gone that route. It might be that it's just cheaper to go along a lower incline.

While those reasons may all make sense to us in theory, in practice, as keen perambulatory people, we might want to take issues into our own hands. If the path isn't going exactly the way we want it to, we might simply step off it. We might make a break for it. Run free.

Take a park, for example. A small park might have pavements round its four corners to maximise grass space for sunbathing and picnicking and heavy petting. To make sure there is enough space for people running away from hoverflies.

Some people, however, may not want to go all the way around the park. They might want to nip across it and cut out a hundred yards of their journey. If enough people do this, a new path begins to form. The grass that the city plan-ners were trying so hard to protect gets worn away. An aerial photo would show a new track cutting a diagonal across the square. There might be two, each crossing one another in the middle. Or more.

This is called a desire path. They pop up when what has come before doesn't match the needs of the public. J. M. Barrie (of *Peter Pan* fame) described them as 'paths that have made themselves', but the wonderful man is mistaken here. They're made by us. They're made by people who find their needs have not been met by the architects.

There is a desire path next to the main road out of my town. Whoever is in charge of planning these things didn't include a pavement for pedestrians. It's not a nice place to walk. In fact, it's a pretty scary place to walk. And yet, people need to get from A to B. That's the quickest route, so the informal path has appeared. When the powers that be chose not to make it a proper track, they made the walkers' journey more perilous.

We see the same sort of decisions being made all the time, every day, in politics. Elections tend to be every four or five years. Once they're done, the winners set about doing their bits and pieces, working out what's best for the people. You can imagine those in charge, for example, agreeing that the optimum grass space must be maintained at all costs for this park's primary function, without considering other needs and uses surrounding it – such as the commuters on their morning walk to the station.

The decisions that are made by the people in charge have a huge impact on everyone else. There needs to be so much more consideration of the views, desires and needs of the governed. If there isn't – people simply won't stay on the path.

Here in my hometown of Whitstable, on the Kentish coast, we have a few issues with anti-social behaviour. Some young people come to town and cause a little bit of a scene every now and again. There is some music and some drug use and some drinking and some littering and some fighting. Fairly standard stuff, but the residents don't like it.

Cometh the hour, cometh the council. All kinds of public order rules were slapped down. That's the local representatives doing their job. They were elected to listen to the residents and they duly took action and announced a set of measures that included a complete ban on both glass bottles and disposable BBQs on the beach. For many residents, that meant no Sunday afternoons by the sea with a bottle of wine and some grilled halloumi. Our Australian neighbours no longer had anywhere to throw their shrimp. The choices the council made, in effect, built a nice new square park but added paths that only went round the outside.

In the end the new rules had to be watered down. It became clear that desire paths would be formed. People would disregard the rules – it hardly feels like an offence to open a bottle of Peroni in the sunshine. But the job of a law enforcement officer becomes almost impossible if they have to decide which crimes to turn a blind eye to and which to enforce. If people decide to go their own way, the authority of the police and the council is worn away as surely as the grass in the park. And so the glass bottle rule was abandoned, although a new rule about catapults was maintained. I don't think many people objected to that.

Badly thought-through plans have bad consequences. Councillors may mean well, but they can't know how people feel about things without listening to them. Sure, they can confer with opposition parties, but public consultation needs to be wider.

When Michigan State University (Go, Spartans!) put up new buildings, they don't include any paths or pavements around them. Not at first. They wait and see where the desire paths pop up, then they build over them – the paths are where the people want them to be. People then stick to the paths.

I was a secondary-school English teacher for ten years (spread between 2003 and 2017). That was during Labour, coalition and Conservative governments. In that time there were four major Education Acts and various other changes. Not once were we asked by a headteacher or anyone else to give our opinions on reforms. I don't know if there were consultations; maybe there were. If so, I don't know anyone who contributed.

We were on the ground, working day in, day out to improve the lives and opportunities of the people in front of us. There were hundreds of thousands of people just like me (although probs better looking) around the country with a close-up view of the system, what was working and what wasn't. How can it be possible that we weren't included in the process?

There is a consultation stage in almost every bill that goes through Parliament. It's sometimes referred to as the Green Paper stage. These days it takes place mostly online.

Each government department has its own page on the gov.uk website. They're not thrilling places to visit, but they are functional. If you go there, scroll past the various press releases that tell you how well that department is doing, then keep scrolling down a bit more, and there you'll reach the 'policy papers and consultations' section. You'll have to look closely though, because it's buried among a series of links to other news, statistics and general information. (You can also Ask Jeeves for 'Government Consultations' and you'll be taken to a list of all the current ones.)

You then need to click through to arrive at the consultation you want. There you'll find some information on proposed plans and be given the opportunity to share your thoughts on them. Sometimes they ask for specific people from specific backgrounds to contribute, sometimes they're open to anyone.

The language and layout certainly aren't for everyone. They're very formal. They can be quite dense and confusing. They ooze the message that this isn't for you. If you've made it this far, there's a strong chance you'll give up.

When the consultations close, the government will take the comments away and respond. Sometimes they might slightly adjust the proposals. Frequently they don't.

This system simply doesn't go far enough to include the public's opinion. No government in my adult life has gone far enough. People will be living by these rules. They change people's lives. But instead of encouraging deep and meaningful conversations with all the stakeholders, the consultations are hidden away where almost nobody except political insiders knows where to find them or how to navigate through them. You'd better believe that pressure groups and people in grey suits are contributing. Are you, though? Have you ever contributed? Have you ever heard about a single one? It's not a public consultation if the public at large isn't consulted.

There is something endlessly agile about MSU's new buildings. And they're not the only example. Tech companies – which pride themselves on being 'disruptive' and changing the way things are done – use desire paths all the time. Twitter set itself up and found that @replies and hashtags were being used. So they built them into the platform.

Unfortunately new Acts of Parliament just aren't that flexible. These big pieces of legislation are, well, big. They take years. They're long term. Once they've jumped through all the necessary hoops to get through the House of Commons and the House of Lords, it takes another whole Act of Parliament to amend them. They're there, solid and in place.

With new laws, the paths *have* to be put down when the building is made. The innovative cool stuff built in from the get-go. To get there, we've got to use the expertise in the country. As I write, the costs and minimum standards of childcare are being debated. Who knows childcare better than child-carers? Who knows what paths should be built better than the parents who need those child-carers?

And yet, these people aren't widely aware of the consultations that have taken place. Successive governments have failed to publicise consultations, they've failed to make them accessible, they've failed to make them engaging and they've failed to engage with them.

There is almost certainly a role for digital consultations, if they're publicised better (and trust me, the government knows exactly how to publicise things – it's able to push hundreds of attack adverts out there) and made more user-friendly.

I think those involved in creating new laws also need to leave Westminster. They need to spend some time in the field their policies will affect. A day in a few hospitals around the country, for example. Making sure they've had input from the doctors, nurses, healthcare assistants, porters and so on about the proposed changes. Really getting into it with the people at the coal face.

There is also something called a Citizens' Assembly. That's when people from all walks of life are brought together to debate and vote on specific matters. They're used quite widely all over the world, including Ireland. In the UK, they've only been used by the Scottish government. They exist already. They're there to be used.

Instead, we get an election every five years and a sense of indifference the rest of the time. The government needs to use the tools that already exist to get people really involved, to help them feel part of the decisions being made around them. Until that happens, those who make decisions on behalf of everyone else mustn't be surprised when people sometimes decide to wander off the path.

Elections

Ending negative and combative campaigning

Poor Brenda. When the news of the 2017 General Election broke, a news outfit put a camera in her face and told her of the impending poll. Her reaction was to say – in a very put-out way – 'You're joking. Not *another* one?'

I don't know what else Brenda has achieved in her life. Perhaps she makes a mean quiche Lorraine. Maybe she can solve a Rubik's Cube in under a minute. Her Pictionary game could be on point. But, alas, she will always be Brenda from Bristol who couldn't believe there was to be yet another election.

I hate to say it, but she's got a point. Elections are awful. The absolute state of them. There is always the possibility of a campaigner knocking on your door and you having to be polite, but if you leave the house it's even worse – a constant barrage of exhausting political messaging. You've got stalls on the high street, posters on the walls, discarded leaflets floating down the canal.

Duck into the shop to pick up a Wham! bar and you're confronted with piles of politicised newspapers. The newspapers are the worst. Massive headlines full of hatred and bile.

In 2017 it was 'Don't chuck Britain in the Cor-bin' or 'Lies, damned lies and Theresa May'. In 2019 it was 'Corbyn plot to drag UK back to the 1970s' and 'How can anyone trust [Johnson]?'

It's not just the largest two parties for whom this vitriol is reserved. While in general the papers confine their contempt for other party leaders to the middle pages, in 2015, the *Daily Mail* dedicated its front page to describing Nicola Sturgeon as the 'Most dangerous woman in Britain'.

It shouldn't be this way. It should never have been this way.

Let's say (somewhat optimistically) you have eight decades of adult life. As General Elections are held every five years, that means you'll have the chance to vote in sixteen of them. Maybe a few more with political turmoil thrown in. That's it.

Think about the planning so many people put into annual events. The anticipation and excitement as Christmas draws near. The Summer Solstice. Eurovision. A General Election should be all those things rolled into one. There should be a national thrill as the ballot approaches.

And yet . . . those headlines. Enthusiasm and eagerness are nowhere to be seen.

Let's take a step back. What is the point of a General Election?

The point of a General Election is to shape our collective future. An opportunity for you, for me, for the mutual friends we might have, for both Ant and Dec, for Ellie Goulding . . . for all of us to have a say about what we want.

Everything is on the table at election time. All the biggest questions. What does it mean in today's world to have a national health service? Should we tax the gambling industry more? What does a good education look like? When you cast your vote at an election, you're signing up to a whole set of policies, a whole way of thinking on these important issues.

If that's the case, and it is, then why is everything so negative? Why is everyone so committed to telling the world how awful the other parties are, rather than focusing on what they would do to make things better? Why are so many people more preoccupied with keeping a particular party out than who they vote in?

We know it's not right. The greatest political speeches of all time have been about positive change. Martin Luther

King Jr spoke about his dream. Henry V's inspiring speech before the Battle of Agincourt (in the Shakespeare play at least – the portrayal may well be slightly flattering). Even Winston Churchill rallied around our troops fighting on the beaches, rather than trying to terrify us about how terrible the enemy was.

If we're to build as a nation – and goodness knows we need to build as a nation – we need to find that positivity. A politician needs to be safe in the knowledge that if they can build a positive and constructive argument, it can be taken on its own merits. We need to be given something inspirational. Something we can really believe in. Something to give us a little bit of hope.

Newspapers are so clearly part of the problem. Obviously. Splashing that nonsense in people's faces in shops, at the petrol station, on the train. Setting the tone for conversations up and down the country. Throw in politicians trying to play the same game and suddenly we're in a doom spiral. Deeper and deeper we go.

There is a saying about not discussing religion or politics over supper. It's no wonder politics chat is banned when we're being fed such toxicity. Our output can only reflect our input. A lifetime of crushing negativity from all sides makes constructive debate fairly tricky.

The good news is that newspapers are big beasts. We know who runs them, we know who prints them. We can regulate them. We can pass laws.

These rules already exist – but for the most trivial and nonsensical sectors. Pepsi is not legally allowed to say that it's better than Coca Cola. It can show how cool it is as a company and all that, it can make a positive case for the superiority of its products in the cola marketplace, as long as it doesn't campaign negatively. But who cares what Pepsi says about Coke? Personally, I'm still going to buy a Coke Zero. I'm still going to shudder when bar staff ask the dreaded question: 'Is Pepsi OK?'

I'm aware this isn't any kind of cola war. This is a battle for the future of our country.

I'm not suggesting that people should be forbidden from saying anything negative. MPs and prospective PMs need the ability to flag flaws in the sunlit uplands described by another party. Scrutiny needs to be applied by both politicians and the media. There has to be some space for criticism and publicly highlighting issues.

It's the focus that needs shifting. The rules of the game need changing. Politicians, like all people, will only do what they know they can get away with. They're in a race to take charge of the country, and they're going to play whatever tricks they're allowed to.

I know it might seem outlandish and is unlikely to ever happen but as a thought experiment, just imagine if negative headlines were banned. It might nudge us all in the right direction. It could be argued that as papers have a massively reduced circulation and readership than they once had, their impact is reduced. But just because you're not picking up the paper doesn't mean you're not seeing the headlines. They're everywhere.

A good start might be making rules about front pages during election times. Some kind of 'positive vibes only' bill in Parliament, regulations to ensure that any negativity and criticism cannot be viewed without context. On the inside pages, plans could be torn apart and discussed as robustly as they are now. This isn't about removing criticism or making life all comfy for our prospective prime ministers – it's about making sure people won't simply read a judgemental headline (like I say, many, many more people see front pages than read the inside pages) and think they know the whole story.

You'll have noticed an elephant in this room. It's not the 1970s. Political debate doesn't just happen in newspapers, on the radio or live on TV.

Social media is a thing and it's not going to stop being a thing. It's the cesspit of political opinions. The second someone proposes an idea on there, it's given the judgement of the crowd. Negativity spreads like wildfire. Even fans of the proposal can grow so argumentative, it's hard for their positivity not to sound negative. We'll go into this in a lot more detail later (not least in Nincompoop and Tory Scum), but it's always going to be something that makes people sympathise with Brenda's reaction, exhausted by this political merry-go-round.

Regulating what is said on social media is almost impossible. The platforms are having a hard enough time just trying to remove content that's actually illegal.

The first step to solve almost any problem isn't always to look at the worst examples, the extreme cases. The first step has to be to change what you can, when you can. Having a grand plan is great, but you have to start from somewhere.

Which brings us back to those papers – and broadcast television.

If we can create a media landscape in which positive campaigning is encouraged and criticism and scrutiny is kept constructive and focused, we might all be nudged a little in the right direction.

Wouldn't it be amazing to see election TV programmes where relevant politicians were invited to talk about specific issues and how they would be solved? Imagine if those politicians were expected to find things on which they actively agreed as well as debating their differences, to find common ground and show that not every encounter between the parties needs to be a full-on showdown.

Perhaps it wouldn't get as large a TV audience as a programme where viewers could watch a candidate for prime minister be verbally kicked in the head for an hour, but we'd have such a clearer understanding of the differences between the parties, and what they all intended to do to make our lives better. Our vote would be more informed.

Not only that, but with policies being debated so openly, we'd have something much clearer than a muddled manifesto with which to hold the winning party to account, to make sure they follow through on their promises and plans.

The spaces for these kinds of events already exist. The pages of newspapers, the BBC Sounds app that we're constantly pestered to download, the TV schedule that millions still use. They're there and they're ready.

If we can persuade them that elections are too important for this sensationalised profit-making misery, if they can do better, if they can lead by example at election time, perhaps we'd manage to do better as an electorate. More informed, less combative, less blooming miserable.

Maybe even Twitter would become more open to measured debate. Probably not.

Fake News

Navigating false and misleading information

There is a sliding scale of fake news.

The world is round. It's so obviously round. You can see that it curves when you look at the horizon (you covered that in Year 5 Science, right?). You can see it's round when you look at pictures from space. People fly around the world all the time. It's round. It's not flat. Shut up.

So when you see articles or 'research' that claims the world is flat, most of us know immediately that it's fake news.

Other conspiracy theories abound, some of which might sound more believable than others, depending on who is reading about them: the Moon landings were faked, 9/11 was a controlled government demolition of the towers, US elections are rigged.

I never believe any of that stuff because of the vast number of people who would have to be involved and the level of competence needed to not only pull it off, but then to keep it a secret forever. Imagine the book deal someone who faked the moon landing could get. We can't get the trains to run on time, but thousands of people worked in sync to make a fake moon-landing video and not one of them has told anyone since? I wouldn't have thought so.

As we slide further along the scale, things get a little trickier.

There were plenty of people who were uncomfortable with the Covid vaccine. If they had wandered online to do a bit of research, they would have found a lot of supposedly scientific articles that told them not to have a jab. Some of that research was based on reality. Some of it was just made up.

We've reached the tipping point on the fake news scale (FNS), where it's hard for a regular person to always be able to tell what's real and what is fake.

Most of the anti-vaccination myths were regularly dispelled, but they were done so in the newspapers, on the radio, places that many of the more hesitant members of our community didn't go for their information. In fact, conspiracy theories are specifically built around the idea that the 'mainstream media' is the mouthpiece of the establishment and is an integral part of the conspiracy.

The place that those people did go tended to be social media, where fake news is so prevalent.

'Ah!' I hear you say. 'People just need to be more engaged. They need to read up a bit more.'

Alas, being engaged, being on top of politics and news and everything else doesn't mean you're free from the FNS. It might mean that your tipping point is further along, but fake news is everywhere and it hides in plain sight. It's so easy for us to be drawn in.

In the early days of 2023, there was a bill going through Parliament. It took all the EU laws that we still had on our books and put them into a pot. The government could then take them out one by one and decide what to do with them. The process is quicker than going through each one in Parliament, but the review is less thorough.

There was some concern that the government would suddenly have the power to get rid of whatever they wanted (employment rules, environmental regulations, all that kind of thing) with nothing to keep them in check. The reality is that there would be some scrutiny, but it is true there would be less.

As is their right, there were campaign groups up in arms about it. One group published a long post that combined truth, disparaging comment, opinion and fake news in a rich mix that tips the FNS for lots of people. Among the vitriol and sarcasm it said, 'Grey-haired folk are now trying to rush through a bill, off the back of Brexit, that will remove your employment rights.'

In that sentence are two lies. Two elements of fake news. The bill was not rushed through the Commons. It took a pretty standard time for a piece of legislation. Also, the bill doesn't remove any employment rights at all. Not one.

The people who sign up to this organisation are generally very clued up and with it. They are engaged with politics, especially politics around women's rights. Many would claim to be able to spot fake news at 100 yards.

Yet there was no exodus from the campaign group's socials. Where there was outrage in the comments it was directed at the 'grey-haired folk' and not at the writers who chose to deliberately mislead their extensive readership.

The only conclusion is that this audience had found its FNS tipping point.

The tipping point is often determined by what you want to believe, or any preconceived ideas. If you don't trust 'The Man', you might be sceptical of the vaccines being pushed on everyone. If you don't trust the CIA, you might feel that it could arrange 9/11 for its own agenda. If you don't trust this government, you might believe that it is rushing through a bill 'that will remove your employment rights'.

There is a technical term for this, 'confirmation bias', where we seek out ideas or interpret information in a way that falls in line with our existing thoughts and perspectives. So when you see a post criticising the government, it might sound about right for what you expect of our leaders. You might not take much persuading.

The FNS is real. We all fall for fake news at some point.

The trouble is that fiction is often much more exciting than reality. A news story or late-night debate show has much more vim and vigour with a smattering of untruth. Why debate something real and boring when you can debate something that's made up, twisting the truth into something more interesting and throwing in all manner of invented detail?

Myths surrounding the treatment of migrants and those coming in small boats is just one example. When Priti Patel told the Commons that '70 per cent of individuals on small boats are single men who are effectively economic migrants', the *Guardian* used a Freedom of Information request to ask for the evidence that supported the claim. A year later, the Home Office came back and said there wasn't any evidence. It wasn't a claim that was based in fact.

It turns out that we quite like a bit of fake news. The people online who feed us information like a bit of fake news. The mainstream media love a bit of fake news. Politicians use a bit of fake news – especially claiming that specific statistics (almost always based on facts) mean something that they really don't mean. One of the 2019 manifesto promises from the Conservative Party was to hire an extra 20,000 police officers. They say they've delivered on that – which is some kind of record. They're very pleased with it. Opposition MPs point out that those are the same 20,000 that were scrapped since cuts in 2010. Which means that although technically people have indeed been hired, the word 'extra' is somewhat misleading here. The news here isn't quite as real as it sounds.

That's quite the group of people who need to be weaned off the diet of fiction – and wean them off we must. Fake news destabilises, it vilifies, it corrupts, it removes the possibility of people making their own decisions based on the facts available.

Facts. Clear, accessible facts. They are the solution here. If you know the facts, then you can still dislike the current government or mistrust the CIA or whatever. You're just in charge of your own thoughts and not being manipulated by others for their own agenda.

Of course there will always be people who won't accept these facts are indeed correct. They'll never trust any information that comes from what they see as the establishment. They've gone too far down the rabbit hole. They've seen *The Matrix*, you can't fool them. Let's park that group for now. Let's focus on getting the established truth out there for those still willing to hear it.

The good news is that we have got people who are big into facts. There is an organisation called Full Fact. The BBC has Verify. Channel Four has FactCheck. There are presumably others.

But it's not enough. It relies on people to search for the truth, to hit Google proactively and try to find out what's really going on, if any of the claims they've just read about hold water. That doesn't happen very much.

If we're going to bring down this dragon, we're going to need a mighty big lance. A couple of small organisations aren't going to cut it.

We need to create an entire industry of regulated fact checking. It needs to be funded properly. If we made it a condition of broadcasting that you had to pay a tiny amount of turnover (say, 0.5 per cent) to an independently run organisation that then had real muscle, we'd be getting somewhere. There would also need to be a strong commitment from major broadcasters to agree not to knowingly report untruths.

If they could then work with social media firms to check on the output of accounts with a certain minimum following or posts with a certain amount of traction, we could be spotting these things from the start. It might become a daily habit to be looking out for things that might sound OK at first, but don't bear much scrutiny.

Another issue is that fact checking is boring. It's dull to do the actual fact checking and it's dull when that fact checking shows that the truth is more boring than the lie. Maybe it's a little sexy when a famous person is pulled up for having said something completely untrue, but on the whole . . . yawn. Someone retracting something they said gets a tenth of the audience they got when they said the big thing.

How to make it more exciting so the truth grabs people's attention? Honestly, I'm a little stumped here. Perhaps we could have a few minutes dedicated to it during *Strictly*. Holding up panels to score each broadcaster on their performance that week. OK, that's a terrible idea.

One thing that the broadcasters all have is people who create shows for a living. Who make things exciting for a living. There is a popular BBC Saturday night TV show that's based around couples catching a ball as it falls from the studio ceiling. The game of 'catch' turned into prime-time viewing. ITV had a very long-running quiz show based on those 2p pushing machines you get at the arcades.

If we can turn those into hits, someone somewhere in the vaults of wherever they do these things must be able to find a way of presenting fact checking and promoting fact-based reporting in a way that gets people talking. There are plenty of former members of JLS knocking about. I believe that the diary for a few of The Saturdays might be pretty light too . . .

God

The role of religion in a multi-faith society

Theologians will argue that God is omnipresent. Which is a fancy way of saying 'everywhere'. When it comes to politics at least, they aren't wrong.

Every day when Parliament is sitting, both the Commons and the Lords start their day with prayers. It's the only part of proceedings when there are no TV cameras and no visitors, so I've not seen it but I'd imagine it's all very quiet and reflective. No bells and smells. Possibly not dissimilar to the moment of silence I tried to have with my Year 7 tutor group at the end of every day when Ofsted had told my headteacher there wasn't enough religion on the agenda.

When the day is up and running, proceedings are still being overlooked by the Lord Almighty. The twenty-six most senior bishops of the Church of England are members of the House of Lords. As a team, they're called the Lords Spiritual. They're not there every day, but they speak and vote alongside all the other members of the House of Lords (there's about 780 of them in total), having a say on the bills being passed as well as the opportunity to hold members of the government to account with oral and written questions.

Any bill that goes through Parliament is overseen by the Church of England, every step of the way, ending with the monarch signing it off. The king has many titles, but one of them is 'Defender of the Faith', which has been around since Pope Leo X conferred it on King Henry VIII in 1521 (before Henry decided to part ways with the pope and declared himself head of the Church of England). Times have changed since then and it's now a reference to his role as Supreme Governor of the Church of England, but it's still pretty central to the role. You'll find 'Fid Def' or 'FD' on most coins.

Meanwhile, back in modern-day Britain, we're no longer a Christian-majority country.

In the 2021 census, less than half of the population of England and Wales described themselves as 'Christian'. Just 46 per cent ticked the Christian box, down from 59.3 per cent in 2011. A steep decline. Coming in at two is 'no religion': in 2011 that was a quarter, but by 2021 it had risen to 37 per cent of respondents. After that, we've got Muslim (6.5 per cent), Hindu (1.7 per cent), Sikh (0.9 per cent), Buddhist and Jewish (both 0.5 per cent).

We're being governed by a system that has religion embedded within it, despite most of us not being part of that religion. Despite more than one in three of us describing ourselves as having no religion at all.

With religious attitudes changing so quickly, it's inevitable that there will be some kind of lag. The good news is that it is within our power to catch up.

Our constitution isn't written down. We have no single document that spells out exactly how things should work. A-level Politics students have been asked about the benefits of this arrangement since A-level Politics began. One thing that will have been drummed into them come exam time is that an unwritten constitution gives us flexibility. As times change, the way we do things can change as well – and they can do so quickly.

Problem solved, right? We've got a clear shift in demographics, we've now got a clear dominance of a minority in certain areas, and we've got a system that is designed to be able to change with quick efficiency. So why do we still have these unelected religious representatives having a say on how the country is governed?

A few steps have been taken towards being more inclusive. When MPs and Members of the House of Lords first pitch up to take the role, they go into the chamber and swear allegiance to the monarch. They used to have to do this while clutching a copy of the King James Bible. Indeed, the option to kiss the Bible is also given to MPs, but I haven't seen that happen for a long time.

As times have changed, so has this process. For decades new MPs have been able to choose which holy book to use. We've also seen a huge rise in the number of 'affirmations', when no holy book is used and no swearing is done. The person just has to 'affirm that I will be faithful and bear true allegiance' to the monarch.

When King Charles III took over in September 2022, MPs had the choice of re-swearing. The old oath/affirmation that was given to Queen Elizabeth II was still valid, but they could, if they wished, double down and do it all over again to confirm that their allegiance wasn't wavering in the face of a new figurehead. And when they did so, many MPs from different parties took the opportunity to make these secular affirmations instead, including the leader of the Labour Party, Keir Starmer.

Our constitution has been remarkably flexible here. Indeed, perhaps not even remarkably so. There were very few remarks made about the increasing number of affirmations. Where any comment was made, it tended to be focused on the MPs who jumped at the chance to swear in while speaking Cornish or Urdu or Ulster-Scots. That's the colour people want to see.

Shifts away from the Church of England doctrine are, in fact, unremarkable. Standard. Maybe even a bit dull.

Even the king himself is quite keen. He has in the past said that when he became king he'd rather his title was 'Defender of Faiths' rather than 'Defender of the Faith'.

Sure, it didn't happen, but it's a conversation that is being had and it shows awareness of the issue.

The one area that really sticks here is the Lords Spiritual. Those top few Church of England types who sit in our House of Lords regardless of, well, regardless of anything.

It is true that the thoughts, comments and votes of twenty-six individual members of the House of Lords change very little in and of themselves. It's just another way of privileging people and ideas because it's thought that we should privilege them. It's a voice that others don't have.

At what point do we say that we're not a Christian country? Perhaps that's too big a question for now – maybe we need more than one census to make that call. We have been a Christian country for really quite some time.

In the meantime, though, why can't we update our democratic process to reflect the changing times? Can we not agree on a reasonable number of faith members of the House of Lords and then appoint the Lords Spiritual (and not Spiritual) in some kind of ratio that reflects the religious demographics of the country?

The number itself could be extended from twenty-six. Perhaps it would be easier to bring people with us on this journey if we benchmarked it as that number of C. of E. bishops, although the Catholic Church would probably like to take a few of those slots, too. And then make space for others: a group of imams, a rabbi or two. It's harder to define who should represent people who say they have 'no religion', but it's worth doing. Having no religion doesn't mean having no values.

If we could do this, then we could revisit the numbers every decade when we get new census results. Then we would have a small corner of the House of Lords that works as closely as it can to represent the religious values of the country at large, holding the chamber to a set of values that the country can get behind, using the latest, most accurate data that we have in order to work out what those values are.

Alternatively, of course, we could scrap the lot. Just say that being a senior member of your church doesn't qualify you to have a say in our law-making process, no matter which religion you're part of.

This is no anti-Christian sentiment. I'm not against religion. Heaven knows(!) I'm not one to tell people what they should and shouldn't believe.

I just don't believe that we should surrender corners of our democracy, of our constitution, to a group of people just because historically they were once the most populous element in society. That doesn't sit right. Also, as we've seen, it's so easy to change, to bring it up to date with the times.

There are some improvements in this book, some ways to make politics better, that are a little theoretical or would be a long-term project. Not this. We can do this now. We could do this in a week. Come on, people. Let's do this.

Hope

Finding realistic ambitions to keep optimism alive

Life is bleak sometimes, from the deeply personal moments of despair we all feel from time to time to the international crises we find ourselves stuck in. The impossibility of facing the alarm in the morning combined with the impossibility of tackling climate change. As I write, the newspapers are filled with stories about two separate missing people, the murder of a teenager and thousands stuck under the rubble of an earthquake. It's unrelenting.

My personal brand of mental illness makes me especially susceptible to this, I think. It feels so inescapable, so permanent, so ugly. It's not just me that feels it. I have no monopoly here. As Blur told us, 'Modern life is rubbish.'

And so we look to our leaders. We need something from them. It's time for them to lead. To inspire us. Alas – it's not something they seem overly preoccupied with doing right now.

Each week the prime minister is questioned in the Commons. The session lasts only half an hour or so and it can be the only time we hear from them in any given seven-day period. It's a chance for MPs to hold them to account and it's a chance for them to talk about what they're doing.

What a wonderful opportunity to give the public some hope about where we're going as a country. To fill us, the people, with a sense of confidence about the future. That we can expect life to be better than it is right now.

Except, that's not what happens. What happens is the prime minister goes into attack mode. Focusing all their energy on criticising the opposition. Every single week. Rishi Sunak has a habit of referring back to Jeremy Corbyn, whose term as leader of the Labour Party ended years before Sunak himself was in charge. For the opposition parties it's just an excuse to attack and talk down the government. The SNP rarely says anything that's not in some way about independence.

The idea that you are better than anyone around you isn't nearly as compelling as an argument that you are, in fact, good enough and will solve things.

Maybe the day-to-day can't all be unicorns and rainbows. That's the reality of life. Problems need fixing.

A few million quid to plug whichever hole needs plugging isn't especially glamorous, but still needs doing. But we do also need some moments of inspiration to cling to. A window looking out of the bleakness would be enough, I think.

In early 2023 there was a week or so with no Parliament. Both Sunak and Starmer held press conferences about the state of the country and their plans. Oddly, both were in the exact same place: Here East, a science and technology site in the 2012 Olympic Village. It's a place dedicated to striving for a better future. It's clearly a venue for hope.

You'd expect these speeches to give us some straws to clutch onto when looking at the years ahead. For fans of a chink of light, both speeches started well.

From Sunak there was 'changing our country . . . and building a better future for our children and grandchildren. A future that restores optimism, hope and pride in Britain.'

Starmer told the audience, '2023 marks a new chapter for Britain, with a new king to be crowned in May. We must look forward with hope. But for hope to flourish, Britain needs change.' He went pretty big on 'hope', using the word nine times.

The hope that he was talking about turned out to be a little technical and specific in the end. Pretty limited in its scope. We got talk of devolution, Brexit and quite a bit of bashing the government. There was a detailed and hopeful policy of 100 per cent clean power generation by 2030.

But overall it didn't feel like a moment for supporters to leap out of their seats and start singing 'Sweet Caroline'.

Sunak was much more detailed, perhaps as you'd expect from a sitting prime minister rather than a leader of the opposition. He had five pledges he wanted to be judged on by the end of the year.

If a speech starts by promising optimism and hope before setting out a series of pledges, you might get pretty excited about what these pledges are going to be. I can only apologise for the ensuing disappointment. The five pledges were halving inflation, growing the economy, tackling the national debt, reducing NHS waiting lists and stopping small boats arriving on our shores. Key tasks in the day-to-day running of a country? Sure. Optimism, hope and pride in Britain? Not really.

As with Starmer's specific and limited missions, these were belated promises to patch up some of our current issues. We're being sold a jumper when the heating is broken.

This hope-restricted diet is no fun. We get so little in the weekly cycle; we get so little in the year. Where are we supposed to go?

You'd better believe it's what we want. In 2008, Barack Obama's presidential campaign ran on the idea. The campaign slogan? 'Change we can believe in.' The chant? 'Yes, we can.' The single word on the iconic poster from that campaign? Hope. The result? Obama won 10 million more votes than the previous Democrat candidate, four years before.

It's not just America. In 1997 the UK was promised something new. We were promised 'New Labour, New Britain'. We don't do campaigns in the same slick way as they do in America, but Labour did have a song: 'Things Can Only Get Better'. The country went for it in a big way. Labour won 43.2 per cent of the vote – up from 34.4 per cent five years before. They won 418 seats – more than anyone in modern times.

Lots of chapters in this book discuss concrete changes. More regulation here, more clarity there. This one is different. We can't demand a quota of hope. We can't take to the streets and call on our leaders for a speech that we can get behind. But it's still worth flagging, I think.

There is more to it. Of course there is more to it. We need to fix so many problems. We need to sort out the economy and create a sustainable, safe and fair migration policy. Rhetoric and shiny lights aren't going to feed our hungry children.

But we also want to be given a reason to climb on board a ship. We want to buy a ticket for that journey. We want to believe in things. We want passion and love. We want to dream.

It's the same with my head. It's broken. I need to do therapy, I need to take the drugs, I need to see the various medical professionals lucky enough to have me on their lists. It's boring and it's continuous and it doesn't always make everything better all at once.

I need to keep up with all of that. But I also really need to know that there is hope for the future.

Interference

Government involvement in private lives

We are not free to do what we want to do.

That's especially true if you're under eighteen. At that tender age, you can't smoke cigarettes, you can't sip a nice cold beer while watching the match, you can't vote. Under seventeen and you can't drive a car. Under sixteen and you can't get married or have sex. You can't buy an energy drink.

Maybe that's reasonable. Presumably most people wouldn't want an eight-year-old to be lighting up after leaving school for the day, wheezing complaints through smoke-filled lungs about the quality of their packed lunch and the possibility of sweets on the way home.

Even here, though, there are complications and inconsistencies. Why is a fifteen-year-old not allowed to buy an energy drink, but is legally more than welcome to stroll into a café and order some monstrous combination of espresso, sugary syrup and whipped cream? Maybe with sprinkles and marshmallows just to put the cherry on top. I've not seen actual cherries on the top of these things, but who knows what's going on?

It seems there is a certain level of snobbery about this. Adults like coffee and see it as a universally acceptable drink. Sophisticated and subtle. George Clooney does the adverts for those pods. If Clooney is doing it, why shouldn't we all do it?

Energy drinks, though? They're not sophisticated. They're not aspirational. It's the wrong type of caffeine and sugar mix. It's somehow vulgar. We need to protect our young people from this repulsive habit.

This is ideological. And it's not just lifestyle choices such as coffee – what about voting? What age should we be free to vote for the people who shape the world around us? What makes an eighteen-year-old responsible enough to vote but not a seventeen-year-old? The Votes at 16 campaign is alive and well – and you can vote in some elections in Scotland and Wales at sixteen. What about fourteen? Or younger than that?

Of course, you've got to draw a line somewhere. But on what criteria are we drawing that line?

It's not just children whose lives are interfered with on a daily basis.

Perhaps, while reading this book, you'd like to unwind with some cannabis. You're an adult and surely you can make your own decisions about this. Well, the government says you can't. It's not allowed.

The reality is that you can, of course. There are many ways to buy a bit of weed. You just have to factor into the adult decision-making process the fact that it's illegal.

The prohibition on most recreational drugs can be argued to be just as inconsistent as the coffee/energy-drink discrepancy. Alcohol is a damaging and intoxicating drug, but it's got that level of sophistication, of social acceptance. Ketamine isn't the same. Legally, you can do one as an adult and not the other. You can go to prison for one and not the other. Your peers might eye you askance for one and not the other.

There are so many other, more subtle ways that the government interferes with your life. Yes, you can absolutely smoke cigarettes if you'd like – but the government will take over a fiver plus 16.5 per cent of the price of a pack if you do. You want to see a bit more snobbery? The tax on a 30-gram bag of pipe tobacco is half the tax on rolling tobacco.

Fancy a smaller pack of cigarettes, so you can have the occasional smoke now and again, at a party maybe? Nope. You can't buy just ten any more. It's all or bust.

If you can afford to and have the audacity to go for a pack of twenty, you have to look at disturbing pictures and reminders of the terrible things that smoking can do. A dead body. Sad children. Terrifying eyes. As adults, we know that smoking is bad, we know that there are long-term effects, but we make our informed choices on a product that is fully legal to buy. And yet the government is doing the best it can to make smoking an unpleasant experience.

Of course, you might very reasonably argue that smoking is an appalling waste of money, life and NHS resources. Taxes on smoking aren't nearly high enough to pay for the cost of smoking-related healthcare needs. There are no advantages to society, nor to the individual, of smoking. We should absolutely, as a country, as a government, do whatever we can to discourage the habit. It's still up to you, but this level of interference isn't just logical, it's important.

Let's get more personal. Imagine I'm an adult and that I've fallen in love. I'm awake at night. I drift through my days dreaming and texting and Googling rings. Unlike conventional romantic love, though, I've fallen in love with two people at the same time. What makes it even better is that they also love each other, as well as loving me.

We've moved in together, we have a giant bed. We cook, we live our lives, we build our future together. We belong together.

What we can't do is get married. Marriage is for two people. No more, no fewer. Two. Why is that? Why can't I celebrate my love? It may be unconventional and possibly it's statistically unlikely that everything will work out (although I can find no such statistics). Surely it's not up to the government to protect me from my dubious marriage decisions?

For conventional couples, divorce has never been easier. We now have a 'no fault' divorce rule. The barriers to ending a marriage are lower than ever, which makes it more tempting to enter into that matrimonial bliss. We know we can get out, so sod it. Why not? If there might be gold in a cave, we're much more likely to risk going in if we know we can beat a hasty retreat if needed.

But if that's the case, why can't I get married to my two lovers if I want to? Why is the government telling me who I can and can't marry? Who the Church of England wants to get married shouldn't be a factor – you can choose whether to follow its guidance or not, and as we've seen in a previous entry, many of us don't identify with the Church any more. There are places in the world that will allow people to get hitched as a throuple, but most of us can't choose to uproot our lives and move to a different country.

This might be an interference that you support. You might think that our threesome is fine in daily life, but really isn't suitable for marriage. You might think that marriage is a very specific and special arrangement. If you want to get married, the rules of that game are clear. If you want to play another way, you do that.

These attitudes can change over time. Same-sex marriage was illegal. Now it's not. The Church of England still doesn't perform same-sex marriages in its churches, but it will now bless the marriages once they've been done.

It's also possible that you support this interference because it protects the vulnerable. Perhaps it's unlikely that all three members of our little love nest are equally in love with each other. Emotions are tricky. The rules and the interference might be justified that way.

Whether you think government interference in our lives in these examples is justified or not, it is all around us. Just have a look on your next trip to the supermarket. There are age restrictions, cigarettes have to be hidden behind a screen (we're not even allowed to casually look at them), sugary foods are not allowed to be displayed near the entrance or tills. The entire building is filled, top to toe, with restrictions, rules and interference.

The point isn't that threesomes should be able to make it official. The point isn't that we should encourage young people to mainline Monster. The point is that all of these restrictions are ideological. They are all political. There is a choice, and it's a choice we need to make, and possibly occasionally review to see if we still agree with those choices in a fast-changing world. Because some of them have huge implications for our everyday lives.

If we are to trust the people we elect to make such decisions, they need to be clear from the outset what their stance is on policies that go beyond governing the country and will change the choices we can make about our private lives.

The 2019 Conservative Party manifesto, for example, didn't include an 'obesity strategy'. I'm not a fan of the word obese, and it turns out they aren't either. It didn't come up a single time in the entire sixty-four-page document.

Fast forward eight months, however – a period short enough to expect any elected body to now be getting on with implementing the policies for which it was elected – and a new set of rules was announced.

Restaurant chains now have to put calorie counts on menus – you can still order whatever you want, but you will be confronted by the awfulness your body will endure. Supermarkets were facing a ban on buy-one-get-one-free offers on 'foods high in fat, sugar and salt'. That's alongside the sugar tax, which means that if I want a full-fat Coke as part of my Meal Deal, it comes in this little 250ml can instead of the standard 330ml.

There were going to be restrictions on advertising, too. Our poor susceptible eyes need to be kept away from a screen dripping with messages about the glory of Wall's ice cream. As if we can't make rational decisions when we see someone good-looking licking something cold.

The idea that we could have an entire 'obesity strategy' forced on us, which nobody had the opportunity to vote for or against just eight months before – it's just not right.

In the end, some of these restrictions didn't happen. The pandemic pitched up and was followed swiftly by the cost-of-living crisis. Plus a couple of new prime ministers.

One of Liz Truss's campaign messages when running to be the leader of the Conservative Party was to get rid of red tape, to have a smaller government.

Either way, this is interference in our lives. It's an ideological argument that depends on your beliefs about the extent to which we should be protected from ourselves. As such, we need to agree, as a nation, on what we want. The way to do that is through the ballot box. We don't have a culture of frequent referenda in this country (more on that later in the book), but we do have elections.

From local through to national level, big decisions need public support and awareness. We can't consent to something we're not told about. When it comes to restrictions in our lives, I think we should always be asked for our consent. We have to demand more transparency.

J

Justification

Explaining policy decisions to the public

As someone whose mental health isn't quite what it might be, I'm very well versed in screaming 'Why?' at the walls. Wondering what it's all for. Searching for meaning and reason. For explanations for the things that happen in life. Alas, the answers often evade me.

You don't have to be suffering a low moment to ask the same questions of the government. Its decisions can feel equally baffling in the moment. The frustration of not understanding their logic is remarkably similar.

During the pandemic we had daily briefings. Scientists, police officers, nurses and loads of others stood in front of us (virtually at least) and explained the science and the logic behind the government's decisions. They broke down what the NHS was saying, what problems the police were encountering. The minister of the day had clear evidence and arguments to back up their decisions.

That evidence was then scrutinised on our behalf by the journalists who were able to direct questions at both the minster and the experts. Admittedly, many of the questions put to ministers were met with the usual political bluster and rhetoric, but the experts tended to answer and explain as best they could.

It was a time of upheaval and misery, but we did at least get some clarity in so many ways.

Real life, normal life (if such a thing exists) couldn't be further away from that experience.

As restrictions were loosened and we were less and less impacted by Covid, those briefings slipped from BBC One to BBC Two and eventually to BBC News. Only updates from the prime minister got the limelight. Back to business as usual.

Government decisions are frequently made with no effort to explain. It's so alienating for people who can't necessarily follow things all that closely. The public, you and me, our lives are busy. We care and we're interested, but time is tight.

We shouldn't have to watch the House of Commons day in, day out to understand the thought process behind everything. We can't possibly be expected to do so.

One thing that's tricky here is that there aren't many MPs who are widely recognised by the public. Former prime ministers maybe, Jacob Rees-Mogg, Keir Starmer, Jeremy Corbyn . . . that's possibly it. At the time of writing none of them is actually in the government. And so the duty to get out and explain things falls on near-anonymous, largely unrecognised, minor public figures. If they fail to do so, a lack of understanding among the public can cause real issues.

Take, for example, the decision not to change the government's policy on free school meals. People still talk about it. They say that the government chose not to feed children in our country. That MPs wanted young people to go hungry. That's a pretty big accusation – and it's also simply not true. No one wants young people to go hungry.

The government at the time believed that the support it was giving to families was sufficient to feed young people. It believed that the various schemes in place, including council support (the idea being that the local council knew more about its young people and families in need than the national government), were enough to allow everyone to eat.

Levels of funding for benefits and other pots of money to support people are hugely political and divisive issues. The Conservative Party has traditionally subscribed to a model of low taxation and benefits that supports people in need but encourages them into work.

Outside the House of Commons, however, Conservative MPs never came out and made the argument for what they were doing. Rather than making it a clear political decision, and justifying it with the evidence on which it was based, perhaps along with some independent expert opinions, they simply voted against continuing the pandemic-era voucher scheme.

Again, I want to emphasise that I don't believe that Conservative MPs – any Conservative MPs – want children to go hungry. It's just not the reality. But without any form of explanation, it was so easy for the Labour Party, and others, to wield such accusations.

Who wouldn't side with a young, articulate football player when they talk about their own experiences of hunger when no opposing argument is expressed?

Ultimately, the government conceded and put £396 million towards providing free school meals during school holidays in England. It was a victory for Marcus Rashford and many other campaigners.

With that lack of justification, it was a potentially terminal loss for the government. By failing to make the argument, they appeared cold-hearted and were then forced into a U-turn. Forced to appear to care about people. And it's a narrative we've seen played out in national and local politics since then.

Another big decision that wasn't communicated properly was flying people who were seeking asylum to Rwanda. The central idea behind sending them to another country was that they could be processed and – it was hoped – live in peace and safety (just not in the UK). That's clear enough, whether or not you disagree with the concept.

The justification for choosing Rwanda as a destination, though, was communicated incredibly poorly. It's a country that is often still associated with the awful, horrific genocide of the 1990s. There are so many countries in the world that, as a population at large, we simply don't keep up with when they're not in the headlines. Things have moved on since then. Rwanda is not that country any more.

The official government statement said that Rwanda is already willingly 'hosting and giving shelter to hundreds of thousands of refugees, offering adequate systems of refugee protection'. It went on to say that it understands the need to 'provide better international protection for refugees' and that it had assurances that refugees would be treated 'in accordance with the Refugee Convention and international and Rwandan standards'.

The plan is that people will be able to seek asylum in a country that's safe and that will treat people reasonably.

This isn't something that everyone will agree with, and I'm not telling you how you should feel about it. There have been many legal challenges and many cases have been made against it. The point I'm making isn't about whether it's a good policy or a bad policy. The point is that when decisions aren't justified properly, it's incredibly difficult to make a balanced argument.

Again, I need to point out that no government MP actively wants people to suffer. We have a responsibility to help people seeking asylum that's almost universally acknowledged. It's a question of how that responsibility is fulfilled.

What we need is communication and justification. The opportunity to hear from the horse's mouth. To have a deep dive into what's going on; what we're doing as a country. To hear from the experts who helped the government come up with these decisions. If we understand the rationale behind it all, maybe we'd be more supportive of the decision. Maybe not. But at least we could respond to it with rational arguments rather than knee-jerk resistance.

We may no longer be in the middle of a pandemic. We have none of the immediacy of not being allowed to see our friends and family, nor the unendingly grim data of deaths and hospitalisation. But we're still in the grip of other catastrophes.

The cost-of-living crisis is real and is hurting so many people. We need to be updated. We need to be in the loop. To understand how the decisions being made are supposed to help us. Maybe even given some hope that we'll find a way out.

The climate crisis is ongoing too. All the time. Every day. We need to know what is happening right now to fight the good fight. What steps are we putting in place? What impact can we expect those steps to have? What sacrifices do we need to make as individuals and as a country to achieve that?

The list goes on. War in Europe. Small boats coming across the Channel (if the Rwanda policy isn't the only card we're playing). Millions of people worrying about the state of the NHS and its future. To what extent are we going to sacrifice the quality of service, or how much extra money is going to have to go in? What about the police? There have been so many big questions about our police forces, what's going to be changed so we can regain some faith in the system?

It's not just when we're in the midst of these crises, either. The government needs to make everyday decisions. Let's look at education, specifically the topic of Maths. We've moved to a new system of teaching Maths. It's called 'Mastery'. Most people will have no idea about the positives and the negatives of this scheme. It's not causing divisions across the board. It's still worth seeing if it can prove its value.

There is one area where opposition is multiplying, though, and that is teaching Maths up to the age of eighteen. Previously those of us with a shaky grasp of numbers could call it quits at sixteen. Not everyone is good at the same things. Some people take a 90-degree turn at sixteen and head off to an apprenticeship, solving the skills and educa-tion equations simultaneously. The plan, I think, is to ensure that those people continue to be given basic Maths lessons as well as those studying A-levels at school. That message just hasn't got out properly. There is still an unknown x in the sum. Justification equals understanding. Not necessarily agreement – but understanding.

We've got PMQs every week that Parliament is sitting, but these exchanges are confrontational and defensive by design. They're not a forum to lay out plans and justifications.

A monthly or fortnightly press conference to show what the government of the day is doing to solve our problems might just help us all see those justifications more clearly. The voices of the experts might help people understand more.

This would be followed by intense scrutiny from the media, just as we had during the pandemic. That's important because government statements do need to be challenged. Not for point scoring, but to examine and probe the thought process and the evidence, to consider the alternative options and make sure this is the one we want to get behind.

The opposition parties could schedule their own versions. They could take place the day after. They could lay out the changes they want to see and clearly justify them. Maybe (and wouldn't this be quite the thing) they could support elements of the government's plan when they do actually agree. They'll still have those more adversarial opportunities in the Commons. Hearing other points of view is always hugely important.

Ultimately, understanding the actions being taken on our behalf, the directions we're heading as a country, has to find a more prominent place. Without proper justifications and explanations, the vacuum is filled by fake news and vilification.

Let's find things we agree on, and when we can't agree, let's have all the facts and a clear understanding of the argument so that we can disagree better.

Knowledge

How much do we want our representatives to know?

In 2022, junior minister Paul Scully was on Sky News and was asked, 'How much is a pint of milk?'

It's the classic 'gotcha' question.

He didn't know. He said something about buying the four-pint cartons. Twitter went wild for a couple of hours.

Perhaps one has less sympathy for Boris Johnson, speaking as Mayor of London, who when asked by a reporter about the price of value bread replied, 'I could tell you the cost of a bottle of champagne, how about that?'

These days such questions are largely expected and politicians can reel off prices of semi-skimmed, organic, hazelnut and goat's milk in quick-fire succession. It's used as a barometer of how in touch they are with the public. But is it helpful? Just because they can throw around a few price tags, does that mean they really know what's going on with us?

Given that party leaders are almost universally well paid, they don't need to know how much a pint of milk costs. Generally, they'll whip round the shop, throwing what they need in the trolley, and pay the bill at the end without much thought. We wouldn't expect them to be doing the maths as they go, weighing up if they can afford to buy both ginger and garlic. They might have had to do so in the past; they might not.

Perhaps they should know these things so that they can work out what a reasonable level of Universal Credit might be, or to understand the cost-of-living crisis in a real way.

The reality is they can't. Not really. Unless you're going through it or have been through tough, tough times, it's almost impossible to know what that's really like. We can talk about the horrors of people having to choose between heating and eating, but being faced with those sorts of decisions is very different to talking about it with a full belly and a warm home to go back to.

The levels of benefits, too, are impossibly difficult for a single MP to devise themselves. You can't walk around the shop with a calculator, looking at the price of basic pasta, cheap margarine and a loaf of bread. That's just not how to do it. So, knowing the cost of a few individual items doesn't really help them at all when it comes to doing their job.

Someone who volunteers at a food bank once told me that they really struggle with people who are gluten-free. Almost nobody donates gluten-free food. It's not, apparently, something that most people think about. Gluten-free food, though, is almost always more expensive than its wheaty alternative. This isn't a fad diet, it's a serious health problem. It's not in the food bank and it's not affordable in the shop. The solution that's been found is to buy gluten-free food using donations so that they can help more people. That requires financial support as well as food support, which is difficult.

Nobody in the country wants people to be using food banks. Nobody wants the food banks to have to use donations to give people the food they need. The price of milk is irrelevant here. There is no one size fits all. Some people need to have a gluten-free diet. Others have dairy allergies. In fact, there are a hundred and one things we could be allergic to. Value bread just isn't possible for everyone.

An MP's job – and this is especially true when MPs have a ministerial role – is to look at options and make decisions. They are in the role to deliver the political agenda and ensure that the promises made at election time become reality. In this specific case they need to decide how to best support the most vulnerable in our society. They have to balance the various needs and work out the best policies.

We've established that it's not possible to wander round the supermarket to make these decisions. That doesn't work. They need to be given real-world choices, between which they can select a path forward. These choices are presented by civil servants.

The term 'civil servant' is often much maligned. It's seen as synonymous with grey men in suits doing boring jobs with little purpose. During the strikes in 2023 (which are still ongoing at the time of writing), the media was full of stories about nurses, train drivers and teachers. There was a huge debate around them. When roughly 100,000 civil servants walked out, there seemed to be a collective shrug. Nobody cared. Poor civil servants.

They do an incredible job, though – they have all the knowledge. The details, the research, the understanding. That is all then passed on to the politicians so that they can make the decisions that will shape the country in the way they want. In the way that the electorate asked them to shape it.

Of course, some politicians are also involved because they have important knowledge too. The members of the House of Lords are selected because they are experts on particular topics. The most famous of them tend to be retired members of the House of Commons and, yes, there are lots of them. Their expertise tends to be in politics and Parliament, but there are others with more specialist knowledge. They're the ones you probably haven't heard of.

Take Julia King. She's Baroness Brown of Cambridge. If you want an engineering ninja on your side, she's the one. She's got a PhD in 'fracture mechanics' (no, I'm not sure either) from Cambridge. She was doing clever things at Rolls-Royce before I was born. She ran Engineering at Imperial College. She doesn't have a political party. She's been chosen because, goodness me, she knows her stuff.

She also doesn't attend every day. Members of the House of Lords don't get paid for their time. They turn up to give their knowledge for free, although on days they do pitch in they can claim expenses for accommodation and food. Baroness Brown voted on just seven bills in 2022 – the ones where her specific expertise meant she could really help and influence, to make sure each was the best bill it could be.

The Lords is full of these experts. That's the point of having a second chamber in addition to the people we vote in. Let's not forget that all you need to do to get into the House of Commons is convince people to vote for you. It doesn't guarantee that you know very much at all about anything.

So there *is* knowledge in the system. There are people who know the price of milk. There are people who know how much it costs the farmer to produce that milk. There are people who know how you get milk from a hazelnut.

There is still a frequent argument made that those at the top of government departments really need to have some knowledge of their own – that it's ludicrous to have someone making these big decisions at the top if they've never been through it or done it for themselves. These are the ministers that run things like the Department of Education or Health and Social Care.

It does happen occasionally – Maria Caulfield, for example, was a nurse who went on to hold various ministerial positions in the Department of Health. The Secretary of State for Defence is almost always a former member of the armed forces.

But mostly the politicians at the top have had very little experience of the areas they're in charge of.

Generally, the rebuttal to this argument is that politicians are there to make the decisions. As we've seen, civil servants will provide them with what they need to know, and they'll use that to devise a strategy. But it is important that they are not too familiar with the sector: how can things be radically reformed or improved if someone indoctrinated in the status quo over decades is in charge?

This way of thinking was seen when Michael Gove introduced some big changes in education (think academies and a more British-focused English curriculum) in the Coalition government years (2010–14). He sees himself as something of a free thinker and a radical. He has never been a teacher.

When his reforms met some pretty serious opposition, he referred to the sector as 'the blob'. A homogeneous group of people, clustered together, stuck in their ways. Presumably he was the plucky hero in this story, standing up for what's right, armour gleaming.

Not only is it not necessary, he seemed to be saying, that someone should have a background in the field of their ministry, it's important that they don't. A new way of thinking – fresh eyes – is what's needed.

So, there you have it: some think that all ministers should have detailed knowledge and experience while others argue that they should essentially arrive at the job as a blank slate.

Perhaps there is another path.

Maybe ministers should have a mandatory orientation period. Let's say two weeks. In that time they are allowed to make zero decisions. Instead, they spend time in hospitals or schools or farms or whatever falls under their responsibility. It may end up looking very much like a Year 10 work-experience trip as they follow people around on the job and just see how it all works.

It's hard to know how much concrete difference this would make, but helping ministers gain more insight into the lives they are changing can only be a good thing.

Imagine an education secretary who has spent time in the households of a range of young people, accompanying them through the school day, as well as shadowing teachers and head teachers. Visiting primary and secondary schools, pupil referral units, colleges. Might it make a difference when discussing teachers' salaries if the minister had been embedded in a school where staff are using food banks?

Or how about a world where the justice minister has had to spend a couple of nights in prison, and not just as a result of some overenthusiastic partying in their student days. Getting to know what life is like for inmates, for officers, for governors. Taking those experiences with them as they make their decisions.

We are used to seeing politicians having their photos taken on hospital wards, in factories, at schools, but they are bussed in and then bussed straight out afterwards. What I'm proposing would be about meaningful engagement.

It's not the same as having years of experience in the classroom or in the police force. There is no substitute for that, if that's what's desired. This system would, instead, give the decision-makers more context for their choices. It would give them insight into the real-life stakeholders.

It might also encourage people to remain in a role for longer if they feel more connected to it, if they have to work harder to understand it when they start. If certain roles are simply seen as stepping stones to bigger and better things, short stops are inevitable, especially if it's easy to transition between them.

The year 2022 was particularly fraught, there were five different education secretaries. Four health and social care secretaries. Levelling up also had four, but Michael Gove (him again) made two appearances in that role, so it's a bit confusing.

If ministers had to take time to get to know the boots on the ground, the grassroots, maybe they'd be keener to stick with it. Maybe prime ministers would want to keep them in place.

Perhaps we do want ministers to have first-hand knowledge about everything to do with their brief. Perhaps it's enough that civil servants have the knowledge, that members of the House of Lords have the expertise. Either way, we need a grown-up conversation about what we do want.

Long-term Problems

The difficulty of future planning in short-term governments

At whatever point in the future you are reading this, there will be some pretty huge problems that we face as a country. Some of those problems will have been going on for years and years – and will continue to be there for years and years.

The future of the NHS is one. The NHS was set up many, many years ago. Since then we've invented loads of wonderful medicines and procedures and life-saving strategies. Almost all of which are pretty expensive. For many reasons we've also got an ageing population, partly because our health system has done so well, and more people are living much longer.

I could have died in hospital in 2022 but, because of the NHS, I didn't. I shall now continue to be an NHS-user for (I hope) many years. The cost of my hospital stay will lead to further costs down the road. I now take lots of head meds every day – that in itself costs the NHS a few quid every month. With me personally, the NHS has become a victim of its own success.

All of these factors combined means the NHS struggles to meet demands it wasn't originally set up for. And so we need to be able to plan ahead for how we can keep it going in the face of these changing circumstances. We have a choice between continuing to provide an ever-growing level of service, at the cost of billions and billions of extra pounds each year, or of reducing the service it provides to something more affordable.

Transport infrastructure is another long-term issue. It takes a very long time, and one heck of a lot of cash, to get a big transport project off the ground. There aren't many people who don't think it's necessary, but finding consensus over what is needed and what isn't is incredibly tough.

Take HS2. The high-speed rail line was announced in 2009. It's cost a pretty penny already and it's still not built. Various cost-saving initiatives have been suggested – for a few days it looked as if it wouldn't extend all the way into central London, instead stopping outside the city. That's because building through London is expensive and this would have cut costs. It would also have made the journey from Birmingham to London take longer than it would on the original line. Given the delays and expense of this stretch so far, nobody really expects the second phase of HS2 – from Birmingham up to Manchester – to be built any time soon.

It's the same with so many other things. Housebuilding strategy. The move to a carbon-free future. The role of our armed forces in the world. These are the issues that will shape our future and that will determine who we are as a country.

Each of these long-term problems needs a long-term strategy. These solutions can take years to bear fruit. That is a challenge when every few years the leadership of this country, and its priorities, can completely change.

The UK constitution is a fickle beast, but it is clear that no government can bind the hands of another. That means that it can't do anything that would force the next lot to do something they don't agree with.

For example, Rishi Sunak brought in a bill about minimum-service provision in a few sectors on strike days. But he can't do anything to stop a future Labour government (or indeed a different Conservative one) from repealing that Act.

That means another government could come in and cancel HS2. Or decide that nuclear power isn't the way forward and cancel any related long-term project. Which makes it difficult for one government to commit to these things because as soon as the next comes in, those projects and policies are at risk.

With the NHS, for example, it would be counterproductive for one government to decide to lower the standard of service, only for the next to try to up it again.

Let's say, for example, we decide that, in order to cut costs, various elective procedures (operations that can be planned and aren't medical emergencies) would become means-tested. Your hip replacement would be free if you genuinely couldn't afford it, but you'd have to pay for it if you had the money to do so. That would be a huge shift. The level of bureaucracy involved in administering that change would mean setting up whole new departments and offices. Perhaps more private practices would start doing a greater number of the operations and so the theatres in the NHS hospitals could be used for other things.

If another government thought that means-testing was unfair, however, or they just believed in universal healthcare, they might try to go back to the way things were before. They would find that very difficult. The theatre space might no longer be there. The genie might not go back into that bottle. But also the amount of time and resources wasted in setting up the new system and then dismantling it a few years later would be phenomenal.

Big changes have big long-term impacts. They change things for the future.

We need to have serious conversations as a country. Once we've had those discussions and made those decisions, we need to stick with them. There needs to be some kind of process (they love to talk about 'instruments' in Parliament, but I think we can stick to 'process' here) that keeps us on a path we've agreed to be on, regardless of political messing about at the top. Yes, things change. When the world moves on, we need to adapt to the new reality. It is still vital that any changes are made keeping the long-term goal in mind, free from political motivations.

It's not entirely impossible to make it harder for things to be changed in the future. In 2011 the Coalition government, headed up by David Cameron and Nick Clegg, agreed the Fixed Term Parliament Act. The Act ended the ability for the prime minister to call a General Election as and when they fancied it. The date of the next Big Vote was set five years in the future. The point of this, partly, was to keep the Coalition together and stop the two parties from falling out, with an eye on the next ballot.

The relevant part here is that an early election could be held – but it needed three-quarters of MPs to vote for it. This set an important precedent for a super majority to be needed to make something happen.

Might it be possible to replicate this? The government could put forward a Long-term Plans Bill. The bill would set up a space for ideas and plans that need time to be fulfilled, for the issues that need the support of successive governments.

If a new proposal were to be backed by a two-thirds majority in the House of Commons, that new plan would be given the protection of the Long-term Plans Bill and would become much harder to be scrapped or changed. That would ensure there was a cross-party consensus on the issue. That there had been one of those grown-up conversations about it and a path had been agreed by a convincing majority.

There would have to be a mechanism to change it, of course, for another government in the future to make the case that the decisions of the past were no longer the right path for the country. That's the nature of the constitution and of a democracy – and of the changing times in which we live. Sometimes a strategy really is no longer the right way forward. But, again, a two-thirds majority would be needed to ensure that plans weren't being changed on a whim. MPs would need to sit down together to figure out what was going wrong and what's needed to correct the course.

Imagine we had that conversation now about the NHS. Imagine we agreed that what we need and what we want is to maintain the current level of desired service. No cuts, no means-tested procedures or whatever else might be a way of saving. That would mean we agreed that extra funds had to be found for the NHS no matter what.

Into the long-term bucket goes NHS provision. There would have to be a commission set up to tell (not recommend) the government how much extra cash it needs every year, or every few years. The government would then be duty bound to find that money from somewhere. Both the NHS and the public would have some certainty. That might come at the cost of tax rises (maybe), but that's a decision we'd have made together, that it was an acceptable price to pay to preserve the NHS.

It's not a foolproof solution. The Fixed-term Parliament Act turned out to be a pain for Prime Minister Boris Johnson, who wanted to call an early General Election in 2019 in an attempt to end the Brexit shenanigans. In the end he was able to call an election and won a big majority in the Commons. But he didn't do it by achieving the two-thirds majority; he did it by repealing the bill. Repealing a bill only needs a regular 51 per cent of the votes.

If a future government came in and really didn't want to pay the extra billions on the NHS or fund a new nuclear power station or whatever else, it could just repeal the Long-term Plans Bill. That would then leave every single plan in that long-term bucket exposed and ready to be swept away by the new lot in charge.

This issue is one of the most serious problems that our country faces: the inability to sort things out in the long term. The propensity for policies and strategies to be at the whim of the electorate. The need to show voters immediate results, at the cost of getting our ducks in a row for future us and our children.

Something along the lines of a Long-term Plans Bill would be a precarious measure, for sure; the protections for those fledgling serious and agreed ideas wouldn't be watertight – in fact they might be paper thin. But it's a start and it's vital to start somewhere.

We need a way to force MPs to have these serious, sensible and sober conversations about our future. To make sure they find some national consensus. To make sure they act on that consensus. And to make it a long-term commitment to deliver on that consensus.

Mental Health

A service in crisis

Physical health is easy. We know what the body should do when it's healthy. We've got charts and we've got scales. We've examined our physical selves down to the tiniest, tiniest pieces – we're currently mapping genomes. Which means we can tell pretty easily when a problem arises.

When something does go wrong there are a multitude of physical examinations available: CAT scans, MRI scans, X-rays. A bit of an accident? No worries, we'll stick you in a machine that can see your bones. If necessary we can put your leg in a cast until it's better. We've got crutches and wheelchairs to keep you going in the meantime. Many cancers are now treatable. We've got drugs that have transformed AIDS from a severely life-threatening virus to one that can be managed long term.

We can identify and try to cure or manage so many different issues with our bodies. It's really quite remarkable.

This is a simplification. It's not always easy. Not by a long shot. People go through hell. Lives are lost in the most tragic of circumstances. The pain is real and the tragedies are real.

When it comes to mental health, though, things are a lot more complicated. This starts with the basic lack of charts and scales. Our minds work in ways that we still don't really understand. You can't go into a machine and have a scan and see clearly what the issue might be.

Instead we need to spend prolonged time with senior medical professionals talking through and examining symptoms, discussing behaviours and thoughts. At the end of this process, it's possible that you'll be diagnosed. Maybe. That diagnosis might be the correct one or it might be added to or amended further down the road. Any kind of diagnosis is based on judgement and interpretation as well as cold, hard medical evidence.

If diagnoses are hard, trying to find a route to a cure or effective management is even harder. That battle is magnified by the limited range of solutions. Generally, it comes down to medication and talking therapies. I take a drug called lithium. It's been around for a long time now as a treatment for bipolar disorder. Nobody knows how it works. It just does. Sometimes. All the levers that can be pulled here are trial and error.

Even if you get to that point, there is no clear endgame of 'wellness'.

Our minds are not uniform. Our mental illnesses are not uniform. For example, one might look at suicidal ideation as a clear symptom of mental illness. That's the act of considering suicide. Even here, it's a tricky issue, because people experience suicidal thoughts in very different ways.

There's a spectrum: at one end of the scale is making clear plans to end one's life and potentially going through with it. It can completely fill each and every waking minute. An all-encompassing yearning. At the other end is just occasionally, in a low moment, wishing you could bow out of the world. No plans, no intention of going down that path, just a desire not to be here any more.

Does the latter – the occasional thoughts – mean you're mentally ill, or can people without any form of mental illness also feel that way? Can we even begin to determine who is ill in any kind of authoritative way? Everyone has emotions that are hard to deal with at times.

For me, things first started going seriously downhill when I was ten. By the time I was in my teens, things had gone quite far off the rails. I don't know if teachers at my primary and secondary schools noticed and didn't choose to do anything or if they were simply oblivious. I was so angry at this point, perhaps they were a little intimidated by the idea of getting involved. It was the 1990s after all.

That doesn't sound all that long ago, but ideas around mental health were very, very different back then. The idea that boys don't cry was real. As a teenager I felt it to be real. (I also did a lot of crying, in secret.) Perhaps this change in attitude shows we are already on a path to a more hopeful future.

I went through my twenties and early thirties still undiagnosed. I was a regular feature at the GP with symptoms that I now understand to have been mental-health related. Nobody picked up on anything.

Finally, with my career and my marriage disappearing in flames around me, I went to the GP and disclosed how I was feeling. He was very caring and immediately wrote me a prescription for some drugs. I felt ashamed and embarrassed and took the slip to an out-of-town Boots to get it filled.

I had been diagnosed with depression. With that diagnosis I got six free sessions of counselling as well as the pills. I had to fill out a form every week detailing my emotional state on scales of one to ten.

Things didn't improve dramatically. My head continued to be suboptimal and eventually I was referred to secondary care. They set about having another look at my diagnosis and at some point someone said that I have emotionally unstable personality disorder.

By this stage I had a care coordinator as well as a private therapist and a GP who kept in frequent contact. A regular little team.

Things continued to slip and slide a little. Eventually, I got a diagnosis of bipolar disorder. The one thing that everyone agreed with, apparently, was that my mind is disorderly.

Is that diagnosis accurate? Maybe. It feels like it is, but that's the thing about mental health – so much comes down to feelings and hunches, not science.

What hope is there of recovery? Some days are better than others. Some years are better than others. At the time of writing, things seem to be on a good trajectory. I've been able to enjoy writing these words for you. By the time you're reading this, who knows? These are chronic conditions. All we're really doing is managing them the best we can. There's never going to be a day when the GP shakes me by the hand and says, 'Tatton, our work here is done. Let's go and watch some cricket.'

There is less stigma around mental health than there used to be. That 1990s world is long gone.

We're better at spotting issues ourselves and in each other, better at coming forward when we need help. At the same time the pressures of the modern world – from the stress of social media to the effects of the pandemic – seem to be exacerbating so many mental-health issues. All of which means that the number of people coming forward looking for help is rising.

There has been a rise in the number of adults on antidepressants for six years in a row: in 2021–22, 8.3 million adults in England received them, up from 7.3 million in 2017–18.

Which brings us to the politics of the situation. The current system is not working. There are too many people struggling in too many ways. GPs need to keep referring people on to secondary care, but those services – receiving the most vulnerable and ill – are too swamped to cope. Diagnoses and care become rushed and haphazard. The crisis helpline that's there for people under secondary services to call if things are going really badly wrong – which is supposed to act as a first defence against the worst of all symptoms – often goes unanswered.

The government has been calling for parity of care between physical and mental-health care for over a decade now, but we need to pause for a moment. We need to ensure that mental health is valued as highly as physical health, but at the same time we must acknowledge that we can't approach them in the same way. As we've seen, the two couldn't be more different.

We've already looked at how we need serious and grown-up cross-party discussions. There is no doubt that all MPs want to improve the care for those struggling with their mental health. It's a problem of which everyone is aware, but action is so thin on the ground.

We need to start afresh. We need to rip up the current system and start again. Start with a blank piece of paper and create a system that supports and cares for patients in a way that's based around conditions, symptoms and individual struggles. We can't base the system on old physical-health strategies. We need to start with kindness and care.

We need access at the point of need to professional care in every community. There needs to be a system of on-the-day walk-in care as well as appointment-based referrals months or even years down the line.

One of the most useful things I was offered was an intensive course over six months. It changed my life. It was experimental and very few people had access to it. Rolling courses and workshops like this can be so effective, though. Just giving people the opportunity to meet and discuss how they feel, to gain a sense of communality.

This isn't a diagnosis-based system, because so many diagnoses are arbitrary and/or inaccurate. But it is a way of bringing communities together, opening access to a wider range of support, and showing people that we walk this path together. A way of understanding our experience through the experiences of others.

Providing one-on-one therapy is difficult for the NHS because it's so time-consuming and it can be such a long-term exercise to find real results and to make meaningful changes. If that's not possible, then those groups and work-shops could become an alternative.

There is still a place for medication – my medication

helps me through the worst of it – but the group course supplements it and takes the strain off the medicalised process.

Clearly there are mental illnesses that do need more intervention. Some people still have to spend some time in hospitals. Some require constant medical support and supervision. Imagine how much better that care could be if we could reduce demand for secondary services by improving community care for less severe cases.

Once again, there is an elephant in the room here. This would all be very, very expensive. The NHS is struggling and a huge expansion of mental-health services would heap on yet more pressure. But there are a few reasons I would argue not just that the money should be spent, but that it needs to be spent.

The first is that people whose heads aren't well need to be supported by our health system. They deserve care and help. We shouldn't ever be compromising on people's health.

The second is that it will save so much money in the long term.

Currently, when things go badly wrong, the police have to pick up the slack. People in crisis can behave somewhat erratically. They can, sometimes, be a threat to others. They can frequently be a threat to themselves. Both those things take up a huge amount of police time. By providing more comprehensive mental-health care, the pressure on policing can be eased, allowing resources to be reallocated.

The government have recently made moves towards this by saying that the police won't respond unless the situation is life-threatening. To make that move without first having solved some of the initial problems may not work as smoothly as planned.

There is also the cost of delaying treatment – if we don't address mental-health symptoms early, they can get worse over time. Preventative measures like the ones I've suggested here could cut numbers needing secondary services and hospital admissions.

In 2020–21 the antidepressant sertraline alone cost the NHS £100 million. That's just one of the many, many, many mood stabilisers and other medications given to patients. I take eleven pills every day. I pay £100-ish a year for my prescriptions. The NHS is shelling out one heck of a lot of money on me alone. These kinds of community hubs could reduce the number of meds that are needed.

I don't think these cost-saving measures will pay for the widespread and necessary care I'm suggesting. There needs to be more investment for sure. It wouldn't be possible overnight.

You might not consider the rise in mental health issues to be a political issue – it's more of a consequence of our turbulent times, as well as of societal stigmas lifting. But the provision of our health service falls firmly into the political sphere – and our mental health services are in crisis.

I have lived through the current system. It's not good enough. We need our politicians to make it better. This simply can't continue to be another topic for onstage rhetoric from virtue-signalling politicians.

Nincompoop

Tackling the language of hate

When Liz Truss was running for election to become the leader of the Conservative Party (and prime minister), GB News interviewed various people about her and then created a word cloud of responses. It wasn't massively positive. One of the prominent words – and the reason why this light-hearted post wasn't shared on Simple Politics – was the rudest of all swear words. You know the one. It begins with 'C'.

At this point her brief premiership seems to be a distant memory. That viciousness, that vindictiveness, that abusive language, though, hasn't faded at all.

It's everywhere. All the time.

Former Prime Minister Boris Johnson has a story that he wheels out from time to time. It's something of a party piece. He was in a park, either on a bike or running, and someone called him a 'wanker'. His response was to think what a 'wonderful country' this is, that someone is able to say that to him, that they have the access and the freedom of speech. He is showing how above it all he is and what thick skin he has.

To what extent he really can shrug it all off so nonchalantly is unclear, but the severity of this kind of abuse is certainly hugely damaging to his MP colleagues.

When former minister Nadine Dorries announced she wouldn't stand at the next General Election, she told *The Times*, 'I would ask no woman to stand in politics because of the negative stuff that comes with being a female politician in today's social-media, internet-enabled world.'

At the launch of the Jo Cox Civility Commission, a few different MPs from the Conservative and Labour Party shared their experiences.

Alex Davies-Jones said, 'Since being elected in 2019 I have been the target of death threats, rape threats and constant online abuse.'

Virginia Crosbie added, 'Public life and our democracy are in crisis because of intimidation and threats, especially when it comes to social media and online, where a wild-west mentality prevails.'

Stuart Andrew echoed both when he said, 'But aggressive and abusive behaviour is hard to deal with, and death threats are becoming far too commonplace.'

Politicians suffer the very worst verbal abuse imaginable. It's everywhere online, it's in the street, it's in the constituency, it's in Westminster.

The threats are even worse: threats of violence, rape, murder. It's impossible to know which are real and which aren't.

In recent years two MPs have been killed. Jo Cox (after whom that Commission is named) and Sir David Amess. None of this is a joke. None of this is an anecdote. Their deaths are a scar marked indelibly on the politics of the twenty-first century.

Let's go back to Liz Truss. That word cloud that had the C-word so prominently featured also included 'bitch', 'stupid', 'thick' and 'twat'. Even ignoring the personal hurt and pain from constantly being described in this fashion, this isn't a way for a democracy to function. How can we consent to be governed by people whose presence and achievements are devalued to this extent?

This name-calling, this abuse, this destructiveness is so entirely negative and horrific for those that are on the receiving end, but also for those who perpetuate it. Nobody wins. Nobody comes out of it well.

The source of this vitriol is unclear, but social media has certainly made it worse. When we sit on our phones, we can see any political debate disintegrate into viciousness and misery. When that happens – and we see it so frequently and so unendingly – we can easily become desensitised to it. The worst things imaginable become normalised.

If everyday debate has become so toxic, it's easy to see how it spills out from our screens and seeps into face-to-face dynamics – real people saying real things to people's faces. Creating the conditions for a world in which those two MPs lost their lives.

The solution here can't come from social media, though. The companies responsible have been talking about regulating their platforms for a long time, but remember, King Canute couldn't stop the tide. He got his feet wet instead.

We need to find a way for our politics to improve from the top down. To lead by example.

British politics – possibly all politics – has always been based on conflict. When the House of Commons was bombed in the Second World War, there was talk about rebuilding it in a semicircle, the shape that you might recognise from so many other parliaments around the world – almost all parliaments, in fact.

Instead, it was rebuilt the way it was, with two sides facing each other. It's deliberately adversarial. Two sides looking into each other's eyes as they battle for the future of the country. It was ultimately Winston Churchill's decision as prime minister. He was a man of war and conflict.

Today, the apparent highlight of the week in the House of Commons is PMQs. The apparent purpose of these questions is to score points. To land blows on one another. They can be confrontational, they can be mocking, they can be goading. The responses from the prime minister are rarely actual answers to the questions – often largely because the questions themselves are quite clearly traps. Instead the prime minister tries to score their own points in response.

Now, there are lots of rules in the House of Commons. There are lots of things that you can't say, including almost all the things on that Liz Truss word cloud. Many of the insults and confrontations are therefore veiled and suggestive rather than explicit. But the overall intent and tone is still the same.

The moments in which one side feels it has scored a killer blow will then be posted on social media. The inevitable sea of abusive comments that follows has been invited by the parties. They've been encouraged. Where Starmer and Sunak lead, the public will follow. It suits them both to fire up their bases and occasional condemnation of the flames they've stoked does nothing to remedy the situation they have caused.

We need to model how to conduct politics in a constructive way. How to solve problems without resorting to such adversarial behaviour. The different parties in the House of Commons are never going to agree on everything. Or even, perhaps, on very much. That disagreement is what politics is all about. It doesn't have to be so confrontational, though.

Imagine a world where the prime minister and the leader of the opposition had weekly meetings to see what they could work on together, as well as debate the areas in which they disagree. Imagine if they held joint press conferences after that meeting. PMQs could then be focused on those areas of disagreement, teasing out the arguments.

Jo Cox, before she was murdered, said, 'We are far more united and have far more in common than that which divides us.'

Wouldn't it be an amazing tribute to her legacy for our political leaders to look to those things that we have in common, to find a way of working together that honours the votes of the entire nation? She preached tolerance and respect, and our leaders so often show very little of both.

More cross-party collaboration should result in more engagement from our leaders, with each other and with the general public. More time talking to the electorate like adults about the difficulties and differences of opinion.

That engagement needs to be a constant focus. Returning to Liz Truss and the word cloud, when that poll took place, Truss had completed dozens of hustings and interviews for the Conservative Party membership, but hadn't engaged with the public in meaningful ways. Into that void pours the mistrust and animosity.

Withdrawing from public debate is never going to bring people with you. Throwing abuse (albeit in a well-mannered way) is never going to discourage the public from doing the same, which will so often degenerate into ill-mannered ways. Creating and perpetuating conflict within the structured sphere of Parliament, elections and the broadcast media is never going to cool the tempers of the onlooking keyboard warrior.

We need to find the calmness and constructiveness to work together and disagree well. We need politicians to make media appearances and talk positively about the world we want to create.

Westminster is known as the Mother of Parliaments, because it's a model on which so many parliaments around the world were based. We need to find a way to rediscover what global leadership in terms of democracy means.

We need to stand tall and refuse to do things in the old ways, because the old ways have created division and abuse. People have died. Let's lead from the front.

It's not going to stop people disagreeing, but it will model how sensible, realistic and intelligent people debate. Our politicians should be all those things.

Oceans

How to engage with the younger generations

The word 'politics' is imbued with a permanent terror for young people. Sure, you occasionally get a sixteen-year-old William Hague talking at the 1977 Conservative Party Conference (twenty years before he would lead the party). Most young people, though, simply don't care. It would be odd if they did.

Of course, that's nonsense because children do care about politics. They care about it deeply. They just don't like the word 'politics'. They're there and ready to be engaged by the world around them. We just need to present it to them in a way they can understand.

Were you to pop along to your local primary school to run a politics session, there are some things that you are bound to discover.

The first thing to strike you might be just how keen the young people in front of you are to discuss and debate anything you put in front of them. They love it.

The second thing you might notice is how curious, funny and surprising primary-aged children are. I have run hundreds of these sessions and I still hear new, intelligent and amusing ideas and thoughts.

If you were to ask them to group themselves into several small 'parties' and decide between them the issues that matter most, I can tell you what they are most likely to come up with.

One party will always, always say that the biggest problem facing our community and/or our country is homework or school lunches. Always. There will then be one or two that want to talk about homelessness. They always want to find a solution, with suggestions like using empty shops on the high street.

The topic that comes up more than any other, though, by a country mile, is the oceans.

Young people from so many different backgrounds are worried about the state of our oceans. They're full of our old rubbish – fishing nets, microplastics, those six-pack plastic rings – and getting warmer due to climate change, and all marine species are suffering as a result. Turtles in particular seem to have become a symbol of the issue for children.

It's rare that, when the final votes come in, oceans – and the turtles – aren't at the top.

Why are young people so aware and so concerned about the oceans? How is it that (in my first-hand experience at least) it's the single biggest issue for this group of people?

The answer is our national treasure, Sir David Attenborough. In a very clear and engaging way, Sir David and his wonderful team have communicated this problem incredibly well to this cohort of our population. Often the TV programmes show us the wonder and brilliance of the natural world, before the man himself comes on and talks about its fragility and potential destruction. We're introduced to the most incredible things and then told that they're not going to survive. It's beautiful and it's brutal.

Many young people see the documentaries at school and at home. The message is repeated again and again. Watching a turtle struggling in a waste-strewn ocean is a compelling call to action. The injustice of it is so clear. It has young people firmly on board.

Not many children of this age would say they're into politics – in fact it sounds a little strange when they do. But when it comes to this issue, they're into politics.

What next? Where do we go from here?

At the end of the politics sessions we talk about this question. Who needs to do what to make things better? Who might we be able to persuade to be on our side on this? We talk about letter writing, the council, the MP, private companies. I try to leave on a high note, with the young people feeling empowered that they can make a difference.

The reality of what happens next, however, is a little bleak. The class might write a letter to their MP. MPs are really good at responding and often do so on nice House of Commons headed paper and it all feels very official, but it's then really hard to engage further. It ends up feeling quite nebulous.

In fact, we are making some progress as an international community. In early 2023 the High Seas Treaty was agreed by the United Nations. It aims to protect 30 per cent of the world's international waters by 2030 – that's 29 per cent more than are protected today. Is it enough? The UN delegates gave it a standing ovation when it was signed, so maybe. It's got to be something.

But to what extent does it match the expectations of young people back here in the UK? Probably not greatly. The political realities that the UN had to wade through to make the treaty a real thing mean that it had to be more watered down than an idealistic Year 5 pupil might want. More importantly, the progress isn't really communicated to them. The signing of the treaty was barely reported in the UK media. If those children who have found an issue they care about just get a nice but ultimately meaningless letter back from their MP and they aren't aware of these (slightly technical) little victories, it feels as if nothing is happening. That spark of empowerment and passion slowly goes out.

Their first exploration into real-world politics comes with a lesson that politics doesn't matter. That you can't make a difference. That the world is doomed with or without you, so what's the point?

We've got to be able to do better than this. We've got to involve our young people and find ways to engage with them on a wide range of issues. There are organisations out there to help.

First News has a weekly newspaper that breaks down current events and politics in a way that children can relate to.

Votes for Schools does, well, votes for schools. It's a platform that sets a topic every week and thousands of young people vote on it. They then collate the answers and ask 'experts' to comment on the results. (I put the word 'experts' in quotation marks because I have been asked to comment in the past and I'm nobody's expert.)

The Politics Project gets politicians going into schools, creating dialogue between MPs, members of the House of Lords, mayors and councillors and the young people in their constituencies.

There are so many more.

All these organisations, though, need funding one way or another. They need to charge schools or raise money elsewhere. Neither option is brilliant. Neither guarantees their continued existence.

The schools don't even need to include any of this at primary level. There is a suggested Citizenship curriculum, but it's 'non-statutory and schools are not required to follow it'.

The government does nothing here. There is no attempt to communicate with primary-aged children. The desire to do so simply isn't there. Nor is there any desire from political parties. No one seems to see the point, forgetting that these are future generations of voters.

Parliament does a little better. The House of Commons and the House of Lords have teamed up to raise enough money to create Parliament's Education Service. I worked there for a while, from 2008 to 2011. Since then, they've opened an entire building. There are good people there doing the best they can with what resources they have.

The issue they've got is that they have to be so completely impartial that they can't really talk about any kind of real-world issues. It's all about procedure – and procedure is always dull. Nobody gets engaged with politics by knowing that the Speaker calls people to speak in the House of Commons. Less so that the Lord Speaker sits on a sack of wool.

There is a Parliament Week event every year. The Education Service is very keen on it and spends loads of cash on it. Several ways that you can engage with Parliament Week are based around Big Ben. You can bake Big Ben biscuits. You can draw Big Ben. You can 'build your own Big Ben'.

It's a pretty building, but I can't stand this sort of Big Ben chat. It's not how you kick-start a lifetime of following issues. There is a Greggs in Westminster tube station. You can get an excellent baked-bean slice from there – a fact that is exactly as useful in terms of fostering long-term political engagement as any about Big Ben. And yet . . . the good people at Parliament think Big Ben's where it's at.

Parliament has all this money and so many creative and intelligent people, but the real-world impact is so minimal. Their hands are so tied by the fear of doing anything that might not be considered impartial. They're fighting a serious uphill battle.

What we need is a mechanism for the government to talk to young people about the issues in which young people are interested, in a way that will engage them. Sir David Attenborough has done it already. Teachers do it already too. They build and run these little communities day in, day out. They create structure and order, providing meaning and purpose that changes the lives of their thirty-odd children. I'm in a privileged position to see that incredible relationship between the teaching team and pupils in so many different classes in so many different schools.

It's time for politicians to find a way to do the same – to show children what they're doing to make things better. There needs to be an acknowledgement of the young people's interest that goes beyond a nice letter that's been drafted by an MP's assistant.

There is occasionally criticism that primary-aged children are too young to be politicised. Well, it's too late. They're already politicised. They have opinions. They care. If they get the message at this point that they don't matter, it's going to be a difficult job to change their minds in the future.

Policing

Re-establishing trust in a flawed institution

There are people who believe that we would all be better off in a society without any rules. That the very existence of those constraints is the cause of our problems, leading to frustration and conflict – and the desire to do things that are against the rules.

Rules, the theory goes, prevent us from being free citizens, choosing our own paths, existing in harmonious communities where decisions are made based on common sense and decency, not because we're told we have to.

Pretty much everyone else believes that we need to have rules and laws to navigate successfully through life as a country and as a global community where not everyone will always agree on what constitutes common sense and decency.

If you're going to have rules and laws, you're going to need people to enforce them. In almost every country in the world, those people are the police.

The police are there to stop us from coming to harm by preventing, identifying and investigating crime. Their purpose is to make us safer and allow us to get on with living our lives in the best way we can. If we can all (or at least most of us) get behind that idea, we're one step closer to a more hopeful future. It's not quite the end of the matter, though. 'Twas ever thus.

There can be huge variations in how we are policed and how the police work. It is a massively political issue. The world of fiction is useful in demonstrating the extremes.

At one end there's Judge Dredd, a futuristic crime fighter. As a judge he has the power to stop, try and punish/execute criminals on sight. He's a terrifying figure. Authoritative and powerful.

At the other end we've got Dixon of Dock Green. Over the course of 400 episodes, between the 1950s and 1970s, he stopped thousands of crimes with his jovial, kindly and approachable manner. No guns, no motorbikes, no terrifying helmet.

Where we want our policing to stand on the Dixon-to-Dredd scale will vary dramatically. Maybe we need an element of both. Or somewhere plumb in the middle. Maybe there is a distinction between what we want and what would be effective in the mid-2020s.

When we drill down further into these styles of policing, we get to some difficult questions. At what point should
the police have the ability to stop and search those who
might go on to commit a crime? What levels of force should
the police be allowed to use? How should the police engage
with their communities?

At a Pride event in Lincoln in 2021, five uniformed, on-
duty police officers performed the Macarena. It was caught
on social media. The next day, the *Daily Mail* reported on
the response, quoting tweets that said 'for shame', calling
them 'a joke', with one person even saying that they felt
'less safe' on the streets.

The chief constable backed the work of his officers. He
'expects' them to engage with the public this way, providing
it doesn't interfere with their work.

What different people want from our law enforcement,
the role and behaviours we expect from them, is contentious. It's incredibly ideological.

Right now, the system doesn't seem to be working
for anyone.

Trust in police is falling. In 2017, 62 per cent of respondents to the Crime Survey of England and Wales said they
had excellent or good confidence in the police. By 2020 that
was down to 55 per cent. That was before the murder of
Sarah Everard by a serving police officer (and the policing
of the ensuing public vigil). And before a litany of sexual
misconduct cases came to light.

On what feels like a daily basis we see more and more damaging headlines. Each one is a further blow to the long-term relationship between us and the thin blue line that's supposed to keep us safe.

There was a time, well within my lifetime, when much policing was done on a beat. I used to know the name of my local copper. Perhaps if that were still the case, police officers could rebuild a level of personal trust, reassure people, offer an alternative picture to offset the headlines.

Those days are gone, though. Policing isn't done that way any more. Trust isn't going to be rebuilt on the streets. We need to find another way. It starts with us agreeing on how we want to be policed.

This isn't a new problem. Both the Conservative Party and the Liberal Democrats included plans in their 2010 manifestos to reform the management of the UK's police authorities. When they formed the Coalition government they agreed to create democratically elected police and crime commissioners. This was a way of making the police directly accountable to the electorate. We, the people, could have our say on the Dixon-to-Dredd scale on a local basis. As the then home secretary Theresa May said at the time, it would give 'the police greater freedom to fight crime as they see fit', and allow 'local communities to hold the police to account'.

The first elections for the roles in England and Wales took place in 2012. Nobody cared. The total turnout was

15.1 per cent – the lowest in UK peacetime history. Not one new PCC was elected on a turnout of more than 20 per cent. In several areas it was down to nearly 10 per cent.

More people voted Liberal Democrat in the 2019 General Election (they managed to win 11 seats out of 650) than voted at all in the PCC vote of 2012. Turnout did improve to 33.2 per cent when the elections were held on the same day as local elections in 2021, but that's not a ringing endorsement.

As a country, we didn't engage with the new PCC role. This does not mean that we do not want to engage in a conversation about the way we are policed. It means we got the method wrong in 2012.

In America, the chief of police is a directly elected role. It's a technically different role from our PCC. More hands on, rather than managing, but it's in the same ball-park. Not only does the election take place every few years, there are regular public meetings to discuss the issues of the day. You can go. You can raise a question and debate the answer. Can't make the meeting? Fear not, it's on local TV.

That means everything is open for discussion at a granular level. A big event is coming to town – how are we going to deal with anti-social behaviour? Unsolved crimes, use of force, methods of day-to-day crime control – they can all be reviewed all the time. Ultimately, if things are going wrong, the people can replace the chief at the next election.

This isn't a party-affiliated politician with some kind of complicated oversight of the police authority, this is the person actually running the show. They are directly accountable.

Now, if you pay attention to news from America, you will know that trust in the police over there isn't any better than it is here. You could argue that it's much worse. There are many, many deep-rooted issues. The deaths of people including George Floyd and Breonna Taylor signify so much. I am not suggesting that we should aim to replicate the American system of policing.

But it doesn't mean we have to sit back and just accept the one we have either.

The status quo here will not stand. We've driven a road from Stephen Lawrence and institutional racism, to the shoot-to-kill policy that led to the innocent Jean Charles de Menezes being killed on his way to work, to the horrors surrounding the rape and murder of Sarah Everard. We're in a state. Things need to change.

In 2022, London Mayor Sadiq Khan fired Dame Cressida Dick. In her place the Metropolitan Police appointed Sir Mark Rowley. Maybe this change in personnel in our country's biggest police force will play a big part in overhauling the system. Maybe.

In March 2023, Baroness Casey published a report into the Met Police, which was commissioned following the Sarah Everard case. She concluded that there is 'institutional racism, sexism and homophobia' and that the Met 'is unable to police itself'. She made five clear recommendations, including: better protection for women and children; an increase in frontline police work; rapid steps to end discrimination; a review of its misconduct system; and improvement in leadership and accountability.

Rowley has rejected the term 'institutional'. He says that's too political. He also said that he's working towards the recommendations. It's not clear where Rowley stands on the Dixon-to-Dredd scale. Does he want to see police doing the Macarena? Time will tell, I suppose.

The Met Police is a London-based force (although it is involved in counterterrorism operations for the whole country). London doesn't have a PCC; it's the mayor who's in charge. The candidates will all have something to say about policing at the next election.

There will always be criticism of both ends of the Dixon-to-Dredd scale. There will always be times when police veer too far to one side in their response to a situation. And weeding out the wrong 'uns is never going to be 100 per cent successful. But for things to change, we need to first work out what it is we want. What power does the PCC have? How are the candidates going to use that power? What can the mayor do? These are the conversations we need to have before we can radically shake things up. And then it needs to be so much clearer what we're voting for and when. We are a democracy which means we already have the tools at our disposal to get things in motion. If we're going to rebuild trust in the people who are meant to keep us safe, we've got to start using them.

Quick!

Preventing the rush to engage with voters just before election time

When the sun rises on the day you've got a dentist appointment, you get up and you brush your teeth. You brush those teeth for the full two minutes. Maybe two minutes and thirty seconds. Really get down to it. You might even floss.

It will make no difference. When you're lying back in that chair with a stern pair of eyes examining those molars, it's not the extra elbow juice you gave them that morning that will save you. Maybe it's all OK. Or maybe the drill will be needed. Who knows? But that last-minute nonsense, it won't do you a jot of good.

It's the same with elections. When the deadline to register to vote comes around, there is quite the scramble. The hills are alive with the sound of people urging everyone else to register.

At exactly that point in 2019, the Electoral Commission reported that 17 per cent of all eligible people in the UK weren't properly registered. That's 9 million people. No wonder there is such a fuss. The group most likely not to be registered were young people – just 68 per cent of twenty- to twenty-four-year-olds were registered to vote in 2018, compared to 94 per cent of those over the age of sixty-five.

It makes sense. People have to be given the opportunity to vote. Voting matters. At such a vital electoral moment, what more important job could there be than helping to make sure that people can express their democratic right at the ballot box?

I do it, too. I was teaching during the 2015 and 2017 General Elections so I wandered round the school hunting for where sixth-formers might be lurking with a laptop, so I could badger them into registering. It was, I felt, my civic duty.

Two years later, I was very flattered to be invited to open an event that was organised by a famous singer. It was a live performance to drive voter registration. Tickets had been priced with an eye on engagement and inclusivity; they sold out in minutes. The whole thing was live-streamed. Some incredibly wonderful people were lined up to perform. It was really quite exciting.

Come the start of the show, though, hardly anyone was there. They just hadn't turned up. The online viewing figures weren't especially amazing either.

It was a good event, put on with clear intention and a desire to make a real-world impact, but I just don't think it did. I don't think a single person would have registered to vote as a result.

Part of the problem is that so much of the effort is put into speaking to people already in our echo chambers. People you know tend to be a bit like you. If you're reading this book, you're probably already registered to vote. Your friends are probably registered to vote. If you share a Simple Politics post about voter-registration deadlines, it's probably not going to be seen by many people who aren't already registered to vote.

Yes, there are absolutely a few people who might need a quick reminder, but people who aren't registered aren't stupid. They're not unaware it's happening. Come election time, everyone knows there is an election on. It doesn't take intelligent and possibly over-optimistic pop stars or over-enthusiastic teachers to point out what's right in front of people's noses. If we want people to vote, we need them to want to vote.

And that is the other part of the problem: even if you do convince people to fill out the form, that's not the same as them actually voting. I definitely got some reluctant eighteen-year-olds on the voting register in 2015 and 2017.

That happened. Did they vote, though? Any of those I'd press-ganged into the process?

While 17 per cent of the eligible population might not be properly registered to vote, when it came to the 2019 General Election, in some areas of the country 35 per cent of those registered didn't turn up. The highest and lowest turnout constituencies can give us some insight into who is voting and what's going on.

The top six constituencies with the highest turnout contained four seats that changed hands. The Conservatives gained Stroud, the Lib Dems gained St Albans and Richmond Park, while the SNP gain in East Dunbartonshire saw more than eight out of ten registered voters pitch up to express an opinion.

Three of the four lowest turnouts were in Hull. Kingston upon Hull East was the only constituency in the country to have a less than 50 per cent turnout. They've had a Labour MP since George Muff won the seat in 1935. The other two are relatively new constituencies, but have both been Labour ever since they were created.

Where there is a story, people are engaged. Where there is movement and hope – or fear – of change, people want to be involved.

But getting people to engage with politics isn't a quick overnight effort. Their attitudes don't change because you've made a biscuit in the shape of Big Ben or dropped a leaflet through their door the week before the big day.

Nobody really wants to have their box-set binge interrupted by a prospective MP knocking on their door. Hustings events are preaching to the choir. The rush to cross the road to escape a high-street stall goes against all the Green Cross Code procedures.

We need to start from scratch here. We need to find a way to really reach people, to get them invested in their political system, and not just at election time but all year round.

The challenge is that as soon as you introduce the word 'politics' into a situation, many people switch off. We have somehow got used to the idea that politics is boring. I suppose that sometimes if you look around at the insipid offerings of the House of Commons that's inevitable.

Politics is a live issue, though. Parts of the process can be boring, sure, but there are decisions being made that affect our lives. We should all be interested in that, at least to some extent. We all have skin in this game.

I don't want to sound like a broken record, but again the best way to engage people is to do so from the very beginning. It starts at school. It starts before school. When young people are old enough to start school, they're old enough to express their opinions about things. They (mostly) can even justify them sometimes. That needs to be encouraged. We don't have to argue the merits of Keynesian economics at Key Stage Two, but we could ask if it makes sense to pay people to dig holes, just so they can have a job. That's a fun conversation.

We need to provide constant, consistent access to political ideas, opening up a world of wonder and excitement, looking at issues at the heart of our country's identity, finding ways to catch the interest of our younger generations. Flags are a great topic to jump into more meaningful ideas. What does our flag mean to us? Should we change it in any way? What would you put on our flag if we did change it?

It can't just be academic, either. Everyone remembers being taught a lesson about oxbow lakes in geography. I could draw you a little diagram of how one forms now. It's a piece of (possibly useless) information that dates back to a dusty classroom in 1994. Conversations about politics mustn't be added to that pile. We can't have people remembering the discussion about how we should best help look after refugees alongside the oxbow lake, in a way that has no real-world application.

And we need to show young people clear evidence that the world can be changed. That's the most exciting thing about voting. When you go into that little booth you have an opportunity to mould the world into being a little more like you want it to be.

I want young people to be exposed to local campaigns too – seeing how things could be improved, having the chance to hold people to account. Why isn't the council showing up in schools talking about local issues? A new development in town. A debate about local spending. Does this town want to allow, or even grow, more of a night-time economy? That's something an older school crowd could really get into. Explaining that one group thinks this, another thinks that. Asking them where they stand, what they think about it. Reminding them that they will be living with the outcomes.

I'm not suggesting this all falls under the subject of 'Citizenship' at school. I've been a head of 'Citizenship'. It's a terrible thing. Of all the words to put people off with. Nothing could scream bureaucracy and autocracy more than 'Citizenship'. I don't really know what a citizen is. Do you think of yourself as a citizen? It needs to be kept separate if we want students to truly engage with it.

All of this rich mix of discussion and involvement, engagement and interest would then deliver these young people, aged eighteen, into the world, ready and able to vote. There might not be a General Election that year, but they'd be registered and actually want to engage with the next local elections. Of course they would, having spent the past few years talking to the very same councillors they can now vote to stay in or get rid of.

Of course, if we just rely on taking action at school, we're not looking at how to start a meaningful conversation with those who have already left. We can't give up and abandon them to the electoral wastelands. They are harder to reach, though. When you've got someone trapped in school, they're right in front of you. Universities aren't the political hotbeds they used to be. It was a while ago now, but when I was at Brunel University I ran four separate politics societies. Nobody came to any of them. It's possible that this was just my lack of charisma.

One answer is to make sure that politics is visible in the spaces they already occupy. Before the 2023 local elections, Spotify sent me a little reminder to vote. That's a positive step – but it's once again more of the election-time rush. Maybe it would help if politicians had good TikTok game, but based on recent examples, that seems unlikely.

Another answer is to recognise that, like everyone else, young people are engaged by issues. There needs to be a way for them to be involved and not to have politics done to them. When nitrous oxide was banned, many were quick to criticise the government's actions for going against the recommendation of their own drug advisory board. But so many young people just shrugged, as if it was inevitable, as if they couldn't conceive of the idea that anyone might welcome their opinion on it. We need politicians to show them that isn't the case, that there is a process in which they are able to participate.

Once we've got that spark, that tiny flame, it needs to be nurtured and cared for. Maybe just having a nation of young people who are able to discuss and debate would help. But it's all of our responsibility to do better – the media, the politicians, the campaigners – to keep people interested through long-term, stable discussions. Keeping promises. Solving problems – or having meaningful debates when those problems can't be solved. Not rushing around at the last minute trying to force reluctant people to be willing participants in the democratic process.

Brushing your teeth before an appointment isn't going to help. Joining the gym in July isn't going to transform your body for August. Joining LinkedIn isn't going to make you an entrepreneur. Trying to rally the public mere weeks before an election isn't going to convince people who don't care about politics to leave their house and place an X on a ballot.

These things take time and concerted effort. Anything else is too little too late.

Referendum

Overcoming the divisiveness of public votes

I love a vote. We vote on everything in my house: what film to watch, what to eat, which board game to play (it's always Junior Monopoly, despite my tireless campaigning for Articulate!).

It isn't a complex system. Whichever option gets the most hands in the air wins. We attempted a version where films were ranked from first to fifth preference, but it didn't go all that well. There were complaints that I was being difficult. For what it's worth, I still think a system that would have let us watch *Jumanji* rather than *Sing!* is clearly vastly superior.

A single-issue vote. A family referendum. Not complicated by anything else that is going on that day. One question, clearly asked, a short period of time to think and discuss, followed by a vote. Not everyone is going to get exactly what they want, but there are six of us in this family and that's just how things go sometimes.

As a country, we vote every five years to elect our representatives in government. Then we rely on those in Parliament to make decisions on our behalf. Very occasionally, though, the public gets a chance to vote directly on a single important issue in a nationwide referendum. It's not something the nation seems to be a fan of. We manage to maintain family harmony during our votes. The country at large, not so much.

Since 1980 (the year the Lord made me), there have been two UK-wide referenda. The first was after the 2010 General Election when we ended up with a Coalition government. The Liberal Democrats insisted that we had a vote on whether to change our voting system to something called the Alternative Vote (AV).

AV isn't hugely different from First Past the Post. The system that moves away from the constituency-based model is Proportional Representation, when the total proportion of the votes a party gets is reflected by the total number of seats it wins in Parliament. AV keeps the constituency-based model, but the voter can rank the candidates in order of preference, the idea being that the winner has a broader base of support.

The debate didn't set the world on fire. Come the day, only 42 per cent of the electorate bothered to turn up and put a cross in one of the boxes. Of them only 32 per cent voted for the change. That's 13 per cent of the electorate expressing a desire for change. (Coincidentally that's very similar to the percentage vote for *Wreck It Ralph* last weekend.) The matter was done and dusted.

The other referendum was a little more contentious. On 23 June 2016, the UK voted on whether or not we should leave the European Union.

Things didn't go well. Debate became savage. Families were divided. The country tore itself apart in response to the question.

There was always a mismatch in the campaigns. Nobody thought the EU was perfect, so Leave could use really clear messaging – 'Better off out', 'Take back control' – and talk about the large amounts of money that could be saved. The Remain campaign, on the other hand, was stuck with a lacklustre message that said, 'Well, on balance, overall, it's the best decision.' One of these approaches is clearly more powerful than the other.

On the day, 72 per cent of the electorate turned out. 17.4 million people voted to leave. 16.1 million voted to stay. That's 52 per cent to 48 per cent.

What followed was chaos. Prime Minister David Cameron resigned. MPs on both sides scrambled either to start planning how to achieve Brexit or to reverse the vote in some way. There was a campaign for a second referendum. The news was full of talk of hard Brexits and soft Brexits.

MPs switched sides, a new party was formed, another prime minister resigned.

Finally, on 31 January 2020, Boris Johnson's government formally left the EU. It hadn't been pretty. We're still divided on whether or not Brexit is a dreadful decision or a decent one. I don't expect these arguments to wind up any time soon.

The referendum on Independence in Scotland had similar effects. There was a huge turnout there – 85 per cent – and the final result was 55 per cent to remain part of the UK to 45 per cent to become independent. Again, there was huge fallout and bitter campaigning continues. Again, there have been calls for another referendum. Scores have not been settled. Some families are still not talking to each other.

It doesn't have to be like this, though. It doesn't have to be so bitter. It doesn't have to be so soul-crushing.

In Switzerland they vote in referenda all the time. In 2022 alone, there were four public votes, on three separate days in the year. They voted on banning human and animal experiments (79 per cent voted against), limiting tobacco advertising (57 per cent voted for it), a stamp-duty change was dismissed by 63 per cent and an attempt to subsidise newspapers was narrowly defeated by a 55 per cent no vote.

The country wasn't torn apart on any of these occasions. They campaigned, they voted, they moved on. Vape companies can't advertise on platforms accessible to children. Animal testing is still a thing.

Perhaps we can't relate to Switzerland. Perhaps they are too mountainous and speak too many languages for us to see that it might be possible here.

Let's look at California. They have lots of referenda on the same day, so you turn up and vote on various topics. In 2022 that day was Tuesday, 8 November. There were seven different 'propositions' on the ballot paper. Californians voted to protect abortion rights (67 per cent), they voted against two types of legalised gambling (67 per cent and 82 per cent), backed funding for art and music education (64 per cent), a new tax on the rich to pay for clean-air projects was turned down by 58 per cent and 63 per cent voted to ban flavoured tobacco products. Over 10 million people voted for or against each proposition. The state (admittedly unlike the rest of the USA) was not forever divided.

American politics isn't an ideal model. For one, the amount of money spent is eye-watering. In the UK we spent £31 million on the Brexit vote campaigns. In California, the gambling companies and other interested parties spent over $300 million on the two propositions that were voted down. That's roughly equivalent to $55 dollars per vote they got.

The US also has (even) less impartial media, among other things. I'm not for a second arguing that basing our political system on the American one would make anything better.

What it does show, though, is that it is possible to have referenda without the awfulness we put ourselves through here. We have deliberately confrontational politics in the UK. Elsewhere in this book I've talked about the layout of the House of Commons, set up for a good old fight. We're told not to discuss religion or politics, because we appear unable to do so without falling out. But referenda can play an important role in politics, giving the public more of a say in how the country is run.

Right now, we have General Elections where we vote for parties based on a huge range of issues. It can be a toss-up. Perhaps you like the Conservative policy on education, the Labour policy on the NHS and the Green Party's ideas for the fight against climate change. You have to look at the big picture and choose the one that best chimes with your views. But you might not agree with them on every single issue.

When we need to have grown-up conversations on things, it's so hard to have meaningful votes in the Commons because of the whip system – your MP is very likely to vote the way their party tells them to. That's not a brilliant way of finding out how we, the people, want our country to be run.

If we could only find a way to agree on disagreeing, we could create a system that allows the people to decide on specific issues.

Take the legalisation of cannabis. In 2016, Proposition 64 was supported by 57 per cent in California and the use, sale and cultivation of cannabis for recreational purposes was legalised.

In the UK, neither the Conservative nor the Labour parties support legalising cannabis (although the Liberal Democrats and the Greens do). In fact, in October 2022 there was talk about making cannabis a Class A drug instead. Meanwhile a recent poll showed that the public is split 38 per cent against to 35 per cent for legalisation, while 20 per cent said they weren't sure.

There is a clear gap here between the major political parties and the public they represent. It's possible (perhaps likely) that a vote would say no to legalisation, but it's worth asking the question. Why not have the debate? Why not allow the people to decide?

If we're making a more hopeful future, if we want people to feel involved, they've got to be given clear and specific choices about how they would want the country to look. I always believe in asking questions, giving people choices and making the argument for why they should side with you, to win them over. Having a government that doesn't do that can only breed resentment and promote the idea that they're distant and in some way 'elite'.

If we're going to have a democracy, our government needs to listen to the people. A single vote once every few years isn't enough for that. It needs to ask the people what they want on a variety of topics that affect their lives. And we need to be able to have those conversations in a way that we can recover from.

Status Quo

Why we need to question the fundamental way we do things

The world is changing and it's changing fast. From global warming to artificial intelligence to dating, the landscape is unrecognisable from where we were just ten, fifteen, twenty years ago. The world has moved on. But, in many ways, we're still stuck in the past.

Punk band Boysetsfire have a song from 1998 called 'The Tyranny of What Everybody Knows'. They are talking about overthrowing the capitalist system, questioning the way we're taught to see the world. They are calling for a complete rehaul of the way we do things in the West. A change that would destroy our current system, which has created winners and losers, masters and servants. For this to happen, we would need to transform our entire society, our institutions and our lives, and create something very different. That level of transformation, though, isn't something we tend to embrace.

Sure, we change stuff. We do it all the time. The government adds a percentage point to National Insurance payments, or merges the Department for Foreign Aid with the Department of Defence. It might make it harder to buy cigarettes or launch a brief and half-hearted attempt to build more houses.

This tinkering, this building on what we have, though, sometimes just isn't enough. Our plodding version of change isn't strong enough to withstand the constant stormy waves crashing against it. Sometimes we need to tear it down and start again.

The trouble is that we're often so set in our ways, so used to the status quo, it doesn't even occur to us to question it. But we don't have to do things just because that's the way they have always been done. We can't be ruled by the tyranny of what everybody knows.

I'm not sure when you were last in a classroom, but you've probably still got a very good idea of what they look like. Young people sitting at tables. Teacher at the front, with some kind of board up there through which most of the learning takes place. The young people will be quiet unless invited to speak.

That's how classrooms are right now – and if you cast an eye over pictures of some of the oldest schools and the first classrooms back in Victorian times, you'd see that exact same set-up.

Of course, they've moved with the times, and we've made all sorts of improvements. We've introduced mini-whiteboards as well as interactive versions. There are bright and informative posters around the room, probably alongside some examples of class work. Young people often face each other in groups of tables. There might be an extra adult or two in the classroom supporting those who need a little boost.

The quality of teaching is immeasurably improved from the lessons of old. Presumably my leaving the profession dragged the average quality up somewhat.

There have been more significant changes too. You now have to stay in education or training until eighteen. You may soon even need to study Maths all the way to adulthood. You can now take T-levels for a more vocational, hands-on qualification instead of A-levels.

The fact remains, though, that many of the basic ideas underpinning the education system remain the same.

Let's look at one of the fundamental parts. In Victorian times, the school day started at around 9 a.m. and finished at 5 p.m., with a two-hour break in the middle of the day to allow students to go home for lunch. In total they had the same number of hours of lessons as children have today.

Although it can vary between schools, usual hours now are around 9 a.m. to 4 p.m.

Is this really the optimum structure for their days of learning? The optimal learning time for someone in their late teens is in the afternoon, so why do we force them into a classroom first thing in the morning?

Perhaps the more pedagogically minded thinkers back in the day really did hit the nail on the head. Perhaps this really is the most effective way to structure the day. Perhaps it's the best value for money we can squeeze out of the £60 billion or so that we spend on schools every year.

Either way, though, we shouldn't automatically accept that it's the right way. If we were to rebuild our country's education system from scratch, what would it look like?

The thing about real change is that you need to go right back to basics. It's not a question of issuing new guidance or walking into an individual classroom and insisting that they update their display boards. (That's a personal example because I've always been terrible at setting up display boards.)

Back to basics means thinking about the big questions. Starting at the beginning.

What is the point of school? Is it to give us the very basic skills we need to function in society? Is it so that we can help create a productive country? Is it to prepare us for the world of work? Is it to provide childcare for parents so they can get out and work? Is it to make us better people?

Is it to encourage critical thinking and the ability to thrive in the modern media and political landscape?

Maybe it's all of those things. Maybe none of them.

The answers really matter, though, because from those can emerge a vision of what an alternative education system might look like.

Is a school setting even the best place for any of this? Does sitting in a classroom all day make sense? Might it be better to spend different days in different places? Use the community, interact with all sorts of people, gaining a variety of real-life experiences?

Why do we force young people to sit through seven or even occasionally eight intense weeks of term, followed by an extended summer holiday? Do they spend that time productively? Anyone who has worked in a school will tell you how exhausted young people are by Christmas. Parents will tell you how long the summer holiday can be, trying to keep everyone full of excitement and food.

Might it be better to move to a less intense but longer term time? Might it make sense for young people to be equipped to attend school virtually from home once a week?

Maybe not. But it's about asking the questions, not relying on past wisdom. Doing things just because that's how they've always been done benefits nobody.

There are plenty of areas that might benefit from these sorts of discussions.

Take the streets of our cities, for example. They're dominated by cars. Cars are everywhere. They park along the side of the road. Allowing people to store their big and bulky personal property on the street takes up space that could be used for so many other things. You couldn't put a wardrobe on the street and use it as your own personal storage area, so why allow it for cars?

Cars also lay first claim to the roads. If there isn't much space, a street might be made one way and there won't be a cycle lane. Is there an argument for reclaiming the space for those who aren't using polluting vehicles? If there is only one lane, should it be automatically reserved for cyclists? A city where cycling is prioritised is greener and healthier.

Again, it's about starting from scratch. If you take the old wisdom (or tyranny) of cars having primacy without questioning why, things will never change for the better. If you work out and define key characteristics that you want from your city, from your community, you have a starting point to try amazing innovations.

It's this kind of thinking that lies behind the 'fifteen-minute city'. The idea here is that everything you need – housing, parks, cinemas, jobs, shops, bars/restaurants, all that stuff – is within fifteen minutes on foot or by bike. It's something that has been gaining more prominence and has inspired projects in places such as Paris, Melbourne and Shanghai.

There are critics, including people who worry we might become stuck within our own small communities, or that some fifteen-minute cities will become lovely utopias, while others are neglected. And again, these cities might be the answer. They might not. It's an example, though, of some radical thinking. Something being reconsidered from scratch with an aim to make it better, rather than tinkering with component parts that have outlived their usefulness.

Can we do the same for the very fabric of our society to address the inequalities that seem to be built into the system? For Boysetsfire, their vision of starting from scratch involves an entire country asking searching questions about who they are, why they're here and what they want to achieve. For the band, the equal treatment of their fellow humans needs to be at the heart of everything. They're using their music to encourage people to reconsider the world they think they know.

Not everyone agrees with Boysetsfire – they argue that as long as the quality of life for the poor keeps improving, it doesn't make any difference if the rich get richer. But those people also have to ask themselves if our current set-up does indeed deliver that.

Whatever world we want to create, we can't remain stuck in the old ways without ever questioning them. We can't be ruled by what everybody else knows.

Tory Scum

Calming political polarisation and aggression

Should you wish to buy a cute and lovely present, you might go to Etsy. As I write, the front page offers birth-flower jewellery travel cases (no, me neither), personalised rose-gold pens, 'dainty' name necklaces, personalised song plaques and customisable hoodies on which you can print a white outline of a romantic photo.

It's a world of niceness and thoughtfulness. If you're looking for a little something for that special person in your life who knows what a birth flower is, you probably can't go wrong.

It also has an entire range of gifts emblazoned with the words 'Tory scum'. A quick search for that term brings up 218 different products. You can get mugs, badges, greetings cards, calendars, T-shirts, wall-hanging art, key rings, fridge magnets, tote bags, make-up cases, pens, bracelets, necklaces, socks, tea towels, Christmas decorations, shoe-lace accessories, guitar picks . . .

That's really quite the range. A one-stop shop for gifts with which you can express your disdain and contempt for millions of your fellow human beings, about whom you know very little. People who laugh like you, people who cry like you, people who love like you.

It's not just the term 'Tory scum'. A search for 'Never Kissed a Tory' returns 1,153 similar results. Admittedly some are really very cute. I couldn't find any that combined this political message with a birth flower, but I'd imagine it's only a matter of time.

I'm not quite sure how people are so certain about this, either. In my youth when a girl was giving me a little attention in a club, there were definitely times when I didn't quiz her about her views on fiscal policy and the role of the police. Perhaps now everyone has a little clipboard they take around with them – a quick test to ensure political compatibility. Perhaps modern apps allow for a more discerning smooch.

One product in particular jumps out. It's rated five stars with 5,502 reviews. It's a candle that says, 'Every time you light this candle another Tory disappears.' Imagine that. Poor Greg Hands vanishing from his Fulham constituency because someone in Stoke lit a candle. Imagine how his wife Irina would feel.

Tory Scum

Obviously it doesn't do that. But what it does do – what all of this sort of rhetoric does – is reduce millions of people into one collective blob. Not just a mildly unlikeable one, but a genuinely detestable one, formed of people who are all awful. Who ideally we would like to 'disappear'.

This aggression – this intense, normalised and specific aggression – is so inbuilt in society that these novelty items vilifying practically half the population are seen as fun and not even all that extreme. What possible hope is there for meaningful dialogue when every time you reapply some lip gloss you are reminded that we are 'governed by Tory scum, vote them out'?

The constant hum of dismissal at best and pure hatred at worst is a sign of the language of the internet creeping into real life. It's not a huge leap to go from this sort of violent dialogue into actual physical violence.

If so many people agree that someone is so inherently evil, if we can agree it's better that they disappear, if they're demonised to this extent for nothing more than their political thinking, it's a slippery slope towards thinking that taking action against them is justifiable. We've seen it throughout history, groups of people ganging up in terrible ways against others that they've dehumanised.

This isn't just historical or theoretical, though. Outside the Conservative Party conference in Birmingham in 2022, senior MPs needed police escorts to come and go from the

159

event. Regular delegates reported being attacked, spat at and chased on their way into the venue.

It should go without saying, but people who vote Conservative aren't evil. They aren't stupid. They aren't being suckered by a mainstream media that hoodwinks them. At the 2019 General Election, there were nearly 14 million people who voted for the party. The idea that every one of them is 'scum' is ludicrous. The idea that you wouldn't find some common ground with them, that you would simply detest every single one of them on sight is absurd.

The fact is that the 17 million or so who voted against them disagree with them about how to make the country better. It's OK to disagree, of course it is. But if we're going to make politics better, if we're going to create a more hopeful future, we need to disagree better.

The first step towards reversing this trend is to understand what the Conservatives are really all about. To demystify this idea that they can all be grouped under the label 'scum'. Let's have a look at what conservatism actually involves. Not all Conservatives sign up to the ideology of conservatism, but it's obviously a pretty core belief system in the party.

At its heart is the free market. That's the mechanism that gives us the freedom to do whatever we want, within the confines of the law. We can choose what job to do, what level of education we would like, how to spend the money we have earned on anything we want.

Pubs are an excellent example of our freedom to choose. In my home town of Whitstable, the High Street has seven pubs. You can choose to go to the Peter Cushing (a Wetherspoon) and drink a pint for a couple of quid. You can go to the Ship Centurion and pay a little bit more, but you'll get to watch the football. You can go to the Twelve Taps and pay £7 a pint for some unusual craft beer. It's your choice. It's your money.

Conservatism also believes that hierarchies are necessary for people to see where they fit into society. They can work hard to move up that hierarchy – Theresa May was very keen on reaffirming that everyone should be able to rise to where their potential leads them – but having such a structure helps us to understand who we are, our place in this world, and gives us a sense of belonging.

Tradition is important too. That Sunday lunch that we share with our friends and family, it channels something deep and meaningful and British. Wimbledon, Pimms and strawberries, when the season rolls round for that kind of thing. They see these customs as an important part of our national identity.

Their idea of tradition isn't necessarily rigid. We've adopted some elaborate Halloween rituals from America. In parts of the country Ramadan is every bit as much part of the fabric of Britishness as Easter. Conservatives have (almost entirely) embraced same-sex couples – same-sex marriage became legal in the UK under a Conservative prime minister. It's the institution of marriage and the commitment for life that matters for a modern conservative, not restrictions about who you may or may not fall in love with.

They believe in private property. If you own your home, you've got skin in the game, which will make sure you look after your area, that you'll be actively involved in making your corner of the world a better place.

There's also individual responsibility. We are largely left to our own devices, but we need to play our part in contributing towards society too. The stockbroker helps to generate wealth for the country, the newsagent provides the goods we want to buy, the ambulance drivers keep us safe. Some people will be better suited to some jobs. That doesn't mean they're less valuable, less of a piece of the rich tapestry of our lives.

If we're all playing our part, then we need to make sure everyone is adequately remunerated. There should be no poverty. We should always look after the people who can't work for whatever reason. We should, though, ensure that everyone who can does so.

Health, too, is a vital part of the Conservative landscape. The NHS is a great British institution and needs to be protected. Since it was created, it has spent far more years in Conservative than Labour hands. Looking after people who need to be looked after, patching them up and getting them back into the workplace, contributing to society. They might disagree on the best way to run it, but they're still committed to providing a healthcare system that is free at the point of delivery.

None of this is about creating an *equal* society. It's about opportunity and freedom.

Now, you might read that and think it sounds awful. You might think that it doesn't make sense to say that everyone is playing their part when some of those people are also having to use food banks. You might think that the idea of opportunity for everyone isn't one that's possible in today's society. You might think that the single most important part of society is equality. It's just not fair to do things any other way.

That's OK. There is no need to agree. These are just different ways of seeing the world, different ideas for how to organise our society.

But instead of any kind of meaningful conversation over any of the points I've (briefly) outlined above – their merits or pitfalls – we are drawn time and time again into the special kind of abuse suffered by people who believe in conservatism and vote, join or even stand for the Conservative Party.

Pages and people on social media who are professionally angry exacerbate the situation. The echo chambers that we create for ourselves don't help us to reach out and try to understand the other point of view, to engage with them, to try to persuade them through debate that maybe there's a better way.

We have an opportunity to encourage a more civilised approach to ideological disagreements in the classroom, outlining the actual differences between schools of political thought. Once young people have a clear understanding of why people have different visions for how to improve the NHS, for example, maybe, just maybe they'll be able to have more empathy. They'll be able to disagree better.

For the rest of us, we can't have our school days again. We just have to try harder. To listen to other sides of arguments – to seek out other sides of arguments – and come to some understanding. The unwillingness to concede a point, the propensity to shout louder to win an argument ... they've just got to go. It's our responsibility to respond in a civil way.

It's our responsibility to see that our money on Etsy might be better spent on birth-flower jewellery instead of hateful mugs.

U

Undone

Why we all deserve a second chance

On a daily basis I am grateful that social media wasn't around when I was teenager. The worst that could happen to me back then was that someone might have a disposable camera that took a shaky shot, revealing some dubious fashion decisions. Only a handful of people would see it, and the printed photos have long since disappeared.

Angry, chaotic Tatton in 1999 was saved from the ignominy of having his life plastered across the internet forever. Saved from sharing with the world a strictly vegan diet that consisted of pickled onion Monster Munch, Strongbow, Skittles and Marlboro. Perhaps I also would have shared badly shot videos from the endless punk shows I used to attend. Or posted shouty rants about a world in which I felt I had no place. Perhaps I would have wept endlessly and shared some of the symptoms of my undiagnosed, untreated and crumbling mental health.

Whatever I would have used social media for, I know it wouldn't have been pretty. I know that I would now feel humiliated and ashamed of, well, everything. And I would know that it would exist out there for all of time. Sure, you can try to delete things – but the reality is once they're out there, they're out there and you never know what's coming back at you or when.

I was not then the person that I am now. Time has passed. I've changed. My head is more in control than it used to be. Those things may represent my past, but they don't represent my present or my future.

For me, none of this is really a problem. I am free from my past.

If I were a politician, though, I wouldn't be free from it. Politicians are never free from the things that they've done. No matter how long ago it was, how young they might have been, someone is always ready to do a deep dive to see what misdemeanours they might bring to light. From a youthful indiscretion to a genuine misstep, politicians can always find themselves undone by their past.

Is that fair? To what extent do we need to hold people to account – and when might they deserve to be given a second chance?

Here in Kent, we had a police and crime commissioner

who wanted to bring in a youth ambassador who could engage with young people in an area where some of them were, on occasion, being anti-social. The point was to find someone who could actually relate to them.

A seventeen-year-old was appointed with much fanfare. She was the missing piece of the jigsaw that would help the people of Kent. Except, of course, it didn't work out. It turned out she'd been using Twitter a year or two previously to say some pretty horrid things. She resigned.

The commissioner defended her, saying, 'I was not recruiting an angel, and I was not recruiting a police officer. I was recruiting a young person, warts and all. I think it would have been absolutely impossible to have found a young person who had not made a silly, foolish or even perhaps a deeply offensive comment during their short lifetime.'

The speed of this cycle was breathtaking. It all took place in a matter of weeks.

Was this a fair outcome? We've all had instances of youthful indiscretion. Doing impulsive, silly things, saying things we might not even mean at the time, let alone a few years down the line. A year or two isn't a long period of time when you're an adult, but it can make a huge difference in maturity and perspective when you're young.

Children grow up; is it fair to punish them for mistakes in their past? Particularly when they're growing up in a world that is so different. Perhaps in this case the comments on social media were too recent. Perhaps there was not enough evidence that she had distanced herself from or apologised for those posts.

There is a question here about cut off, though. How long can we hold people accountable for their views or mistakes? How far back can we dig for a so-called controversial opinion that affects their career?

Politicians are often asked if they took drugs in their youth (as young people often do). This is presented as a big deal. Why? What does it matter if someone smoked a joint in their teens? Does it affect their ability to do their job now? Do we want our politicians to only come from a cohort of people who were saintly in their youth?

In the build-up to the 2017 General Election, Diane Abbott (who would almost certainly have become the home secretary had Labour won the election) was questioned by Andrew Marr about views she had expressed in 1984. She'd said that in Northern Ireland 'every defeat of the British state is a victory for all of us'.

She responded with: 'I had an afro. It was thirty-four years ago. The hairstyle has gone and some of the views have gone. We have all moved on.'

These examples are everywhere. Liz Truss told ITV, in 1994, at the Liberal Democrat conference, that she thought the monarchy was 'disgraceful'. Keir Starmer also once proposed abolishing the monarchy. Both are now firm supporters of the whole thing and celebrated the Coronation of King Charles III with much gusto.

Truss's change of heart was declared as a major U-turn. A U-turn, really? Over twenty years later? Granted it was at a time when U-turns appeared to be her speciality. Early on in her term as prime minister she had announced a mini-budget that would be delivered by her chancellor, Kwasi Kwarteng. It didn't go very well. As time went on, she would change her mind on almost everything from that mini-budget – including that Kwarteng would be the best person to be chancellor. She U-turned on abolishing the top rate of tax, keeping the triple-lock pension, her corporation-tax policy and the basic rate of tax.

Obviously, we do want our politicians to be able to stand by their views for a certain amount of time. A politician who will dance to whichever tune seems to be playing loudest is no politician at all. But there is a balance to be had here. We can admit that things have changed, we can be lauded for pivoting as necessary. We're not the people we used to be. Circumstances have changed. Outlooks have changed. Whatever the reason is. We shouldn't be tied to any masts on sinking ships.

I'm not for a second suggesting that people who do or say terrible things should be able to disown them with a shrug. We have freedom of speech, but that doesn't mean freedom from consequences. Yes, we need to hold people to account, our leaders especially so. If they say something terrible, they need to face consequences.

Diane Abbott can disown her comments in 1984, but

when she wrote a letter to the *Observer* comparing anti-Semitism to the kind of prejudice someone with red hair might face, there were consequences. Her defence was that it was a draft and sent by mistake. She apologised and made a statement withdrawing her words. It wasn't enough. She had the Labour whip removed, meaning that since April 2023 she has stood as an independent MP.

When Andrew Bridgen compared the vaccine rollout to the Holocaust, the Conservative Party removed the whip. He said he was pleased with his new-found freedom and then joined another party, Reclaim. Rupa Huq was suspended by the Labour Party when she described Kwasi Kwarteng as 'superficially black'.

There is a need to hold public figures to account when there are serious offences, but people seem to be out for blood, giving no quarter, for the smallest of missteps in someone's past. And the trouble with this attitude is that it doesn't allow any room for growth, for changing opinions, for lessons learned. It doesn't allow for maturity, life experience, or the vastly different landscape we now find ourselves in with our lives recorded online practically from birth. And it only adds to the toxicity of the political landscape.

There needs to be some leeway, a chance for people to demonstrate they've learned from past mistakes, that they don't have to be associated with those views forever. Sometimes people do deserve a second chance.

Visions of the Future

Why we need concrete plans from all parties

We all have our own personal visions for the future – we look at our many options, choose our favourite, then plan ahead to make it a reality. We do it all our lives.

When I grow up, I want to be an astronaut. I'm going to go to Mars and look for aliens.

When I finish school, I'm going to do a degree in Forensic Crime, become a detective and they'll probably write a dark series about me for Paramount+ that's rated at least a seven on IMDb.

Next year, I'm going to leave this job and retrain as a marine biologist. I just need to save a bit of money and move to Plymouth to make the dream come true.

I'm on Tinder because I want to meet someone who is going to change my life. Sparks will fly and then we'll settle down and spend the rest of our lives going for dog walks and pub lunches.

Once we know what it is we want, we can start putting things in place, start planning in some serious detail. We can make cardboard space shuttles and fly them around the room, watch *CSI*, read about the sea, put 'no hook-ups' on our profiles.

It's possible that an outsider might think your idea is objectionable, foolish, unachievable. They might say, 'Oh really?' then catch someone's eye and shake their heads pityingly. But that's OK, they don't have to agree – it's your vision. If it affects them and they've got a better idea, they're welcome to share it. Otherwise, you'll carry on following your dreams.

If it's so common in the real world to picture how we want our lives to look in the future, why is it so rare in politics?

We have a General Election every five years (in theory). One party, generally, then runs the country for that time. While that party's in charge, it's making changes to how we do things, telling us why those changes are great and the difference they'll make to our lives. It shows how (in that party's mind at least) it's building a better country, a better world.

What opposition parties do during that time, almost always, is take pot shots at the government. We hear a lot about why the party in power is rubbish, why its ideas are terrible and just won't work. You see it every day on the TV, on the radio, online. A government minister does the media round, followed by an opposition MP whose job it is to tear apart the government plan.

Elsewhere in this book we've looked at the toxic culture in our politics. If all we have to watch is one party in government against everyone else, as if it's under some kind of medieval siege with diseased cows being lobbed into the government benches, that negativity continues to be promoted. It embeds that tribe mentality – are you inside the walls or part of the rebellion?

Our media feels totally on board with this. Conflict between politicians just makes much better TV. Boxing pulls in millions of viewers on TV. Chess? Not so much.

What we, the public, are left with is one vision for the future – that of the government, because the other parties don't have to present an alternative. After losing a General Election, it might take a party a couple of years to get itself straight again. The leader often resigns. Some shuffling about is needed. When the new opposition can, though, we need to know what it wants the country to look like in the future. We need it to paint a picture for us.

Where will the jobs be? How will we be dealing with climate change? Is the aim for us to pay fewer taxes? What's the NHS going to look like? Will we still have all the libraries and swimming pools and playgrounds that we do now?

It's really hard to get behind a party when you're given such a small snapshot of what it believes in.

Labour had an excellent set of local election results in 2023. It put out a video of Keir Starmer celebrating in Medway. It's very slick. He says it's a great result, that they're on track to win a General Election. He also says, 'Change is possible, a better Britain is possible.' That's it. Just 'change'. No specifics. Not even a broad-brush vision. This was an opportunity to lay down some Labour values and tell us what the victories mean, to give us something concrete to believe in.

On occasion, the opposition will put out an alternative policy to the government's on a specific problem. In 2022, Labour really focused on two of its policies. It wanted to end non-dom status (a rule that if someone's 'permanent' home is in a different country, they have to pay tax in the UK only on money that's made in the UK), which it says would bring in £3 billion or so extra cash a year.

Labour also wanted to have a bigger windfall (one-off) tax on energy-company profits, which were huge. It said that would bring in £13 billion over 2022 and 2023.

Those are two actual, real policies. The government disagrees with them because of course it does. It disputes the numbers in particular and says that the windfall tax will discourage investment in the UK and therefore do long-term damage.

This is all well and good. We're getting two different approaches to the same problems. People who believe different things looking at the same data and coming up with different solutions. Giving the voter, maybe, something to form an opinion on.

But the trouble with zeroing in on only a couple of issues like this is that it creates a scattergun pattern of policies that is hard to follow. These two specific policies on tax tell us nothing about our personal taxes, for example. We just have two data points surrounded by a lot of blank space. We can't extrapolate out.

And, yes, there are so many issues to deal with it's by no means easy, but there's got to be an attempt to show the big picture. We can then work back from that to understand the stance on day-to-day issues, where the party is coming from. Labour wants to get more revenue from the incredibly wealthy currently eligible for non-dom status? Ah! Yes! I can see how that fits into their plan. The Conservative Party doesn't want to get rid of non-dom status? Makes sense in the grand scheme of how they want the country to be run in the future.

We need solid visions for the future that people can believe in. If the parties were clearer all the time about their vision, it would give us more clarity on our choices at election time. We'd know much better what each party might be doing, what world it might want to create. Perhaps people would support the Red Team not just because it's the Red Team and their family has always supported the Red Team but because of the specific vision it has for the country.

175

At the moment, nobody really knows all the policies until the manifesto comes out a month before the election. At that point, most people already know for whom they're going to cast their vote, it's too late to rally additional support to your cause.

This change won't just happen. It suits parties to be quiet about their plans and ideas until election time when they can spring a heavy manifesto on the public. It allows them to be flexible, and to focus on criticising each other without having to take responsibility for their own positions.

This confrontational, nit-picking politics will continue as long as we allow it to. It's a system that has bred the current crop and they'll want to defend it.

I talk about us having only one clear vision for the future and that being from the government – but even the government isn't very good at it. We hear a lot about immediate issues, but not so much about long-term planning. It's so rare that some Big Cheese drops onto our screens to outline what they want the country to look like in 2030. This is, in part, because our Parliament isn't set out for Long-term Plans (as we saw in that chapter). To be fair, the public isn't good at long-term plans either. We want to halve inflation right now. We want to cut waiting lists now, now, now. A full dopamine hit of an immediate fix.

I can be guilty of that. I did an event with a Conservative MP and the panel was discussing mental-health provision. The MP said that they were training more professionals and

I challenged him about how long that would take. He said that it was going to take ages, but he (and the party) wanted to have as many professionals as possible at the end of that seven-year training.

He was right. As much as I would love to have it fixed now, those sorts of changes don't happen overnight. You've got to start now to get what you need in the future. We've got to be patient for the results. But it does show why we need to start planning sooner.

Nick Clegg was ridiculed on Twitter for a video from 2010 in which he disagreed with a policy of building nuclear reactors because they wouldn't be ready until 2021–22. As the energy crisis hit in 2022, there were people who felt it might have been nice to have those reactors.

Setting out long-term visions isn't easy. But having a clear plan of action can help the country understand where we're headed. Setting out long-term goals and then the incremental changes needed to achieve them. Concrete steps. Clear visions. All communicated clearly to the public. Then when people suggest that the government isn't doing enough for mental-health provision, it can point to its long-term plan, show that it's training more people and demonstrate a clear direction of travel with progress being made. You might still disagree with the overall policy – and that's OK.

There is also a need to be flexible here. It's difficult for politicians to tie their colours to a mast when that mast might be blown off course. Circumstances change. Most people who wanted to be astronauts don't end up as astronauts. The plan to leave work next year might be pushed back. Your dark detective TV series might end up on Channel 5 instead of Paramount+. The new and improved schedule for the bus network across England and Wales might take a hit because of all the trees that have sprung up, which means we can't use as many double-deckers on certain roads. Things happen.

What we need then is honesty and clarity. It wouldn't be fair, in ten years' time, to highlight the differences between visions for the future and the reality of that future. Plans have to change with the times. We just need an expression of intent. A marker that says, 'This is what we believe in. This is what we want.'

Famously, if you're facing the right direction, all you need to do is keep walking. So, let's be clear what we think the right direction might be.

If this situation is going to change, we, the public, need to put some pressure on. Find MPs who are prepared to ask their parties for this stuff, who want to go out into their constituencies with a real vision to sell. To paint a picture with words. Or maybe just paint a picture. I'd quite like to decide my vote on who paints a better picture of what they want for the country. Maybe that's just me.

W

Where's Wally?

Do you know who your local representatives are?

A *Where's Wally?* book is an enjoyable treat. A wide landscape full of people, animals and objects. It's your job to find the stripey-jumpered character in the midst of it. It's a premise that has spin-offs for *Top Gear*, *Spiderman* and more. It's good fun and it's everywhere.

If you tried that with a *Where's the Councillor?* version, though, you'd immediately find yourself with an impossible challenge on your hands. Because I'm willing to bet you haven't got the first clue what any of your local councillors look like, or even their names. And they aren't (normally) wearing a helpfully stripey top to stand out from the crowd.

Were a councillor to commit a crime, they might get away with it because nobody would recognise them in a line-up.

We all know that big decisions are being made for us. Everybody knows that. When we ride the bus, when we have our bins collected, when we search fruitlessly for somewhere that's open to have a drink after 11 p.m. . . . . Our lives are at the mercy of the people we have, collectively, voted for. But we tend to attribute all of the decision-making to the people at the top – government ministers, MPs, some of whom we can actually name. And of course these people do have a huge influence on how we live.

It's arguable, though, that our local council has a far bigger impact on our day-to-day activities and struggles.

In mid spring I was walking through town with a friend of mine who is a councillor. There was a very dead Christmas tree lying in a car park. He stopped our conversation to make a note of it, mumbling something about how someone had mentioned it to him, and we carried on with our walk. The next day the tree had been taken away. I can only presume that these things are linked and that it wasn't merely fortuitous timing that a passing pedestrian suddenly realised they had a pressing need to acquire a dead Christmas tree.

The people in your council care. They get on (mostly unpaid) with making our area better.

As with everything else in this book, you might disagree with the things that they're doing. You might think that your town needs to attract more tourists. All that lovely money they bring in and spend in the ice cream parlours and gift shops, filling restaurants and parks with their fancy ways. Or you might think that the town is too small, there are not enough parking spots or places to wee, that the streets will be blighted by drunkenness or the rental market will become dominated by Airbnbs.

If you feel strongly either way about it, it's your councillors you need to speak to. If you want to see any changes in your local area, it's your councillors who might be able to make it happen.

And yet . . . we just don't seem to care about them.

I'm not criticising people for not knowing. I care a lot about politics. Obviously, I care a lot about politics. But I can't name all of my councillors. I know one of them because he's Christmas-tree guy and he's a friend of mine. The others? I just don't know. I feel bad about it (especially writing a chapter about how we should know who they are), but that's the way it is.

Local politics – and even just saying the words 'local politics' is enough to put some people to sleep – really matters. A lot. We need to show people its importance. To make it feel as vital as it is.

At the 2021 local elections in England, one part of Hull had a turnout of just 14.6 per cent.

One irony here is that your vote matters much more in a council election. With smaller groups of voters making decisions in wards, as opposed to larger constituencies, and lower turnout, each vote makes for a larger proportion of the total.

If you want to see an example of how close things are, look no further than the elections in Wales in 2022. In Bigyn, two Labour candidates were drawn in third place with 596 votes each. Three councillors were to be elected, so a coin was tossed to decide.

This is the way that a tie would be sorted out in a General Election too – but when we're talking tens of thousands of votes across a parliamentary constituency it's much, much less likely to happen than when we're talking about a few hundred in a council ward. Your vote at the local elections really does count.

With the contest being between two Labour candidates, perhaps it didn't make that much difference. In Llanfoist and Govilon, however, it certainly did. There were four candidates – two Conservative, two Labour – going for two seats on the council. A Labour candidate won overall with 727 votes. Behind him came the other Labour candidate and one of the Conservatives on exactly 679 each (and the final candidate was only three votes behind, with 676 crosses by her name). A toss of a coin came down in favour of the Labour candidate. This meant that the Conservatives no longer had a majority on the council. The overall direction of the entire council was potentially determined by one person not turning up to vote that day.

The same happened closer to (my) home in 2023, in Seasalter, but this time the councillor was elected by drawing lots. Labour candidate Charlotte Cornell got the seat and Ashley Clark, an Independent, came away with nothing. Not even a chequebook and pen.

Imagine the power you have as a voter in an area as tight as that. Imagine your vote genuinely making a difference. It puts you in a real position of power and influence.

But most people don't realise it. That power isn't used. It's passed over in favour of a few more minutes on the sofa, a slightly earlier bedtime. It just feels like too much effort to go vote for a bunch of people you know nothing about for a role you don't understand.

This creates a terrible loop. Most people don't vote, so someone the majority don't want wins. Decisions are made that most people don't agree with. Trust in 'the council' is diminished. Elections come around next time and turnout is even lower, because no one has any faith the council matters or can get anything done. The smaller the pool of voters, the less likely it is their representative will reflect the majority views in the area. The gap between the council and the councilled grows. And so on.

We need to find a way to change this. We need to start with helping people to know who their representatives are. One solution could be to put up huge posters of our councillors on the high street. I think that would work, to be fair. If you had the leader of your council staring down at you while you go about your business of casually buying carrots and wine, you might remember their name. Maybe not.

No, what we need is to engage people. To show them not just who these people are but demonstrate the important work that they do.

When we were part of the EU, projects that were funded by the EU were labelled as such. The ferry terminal at Fishguard in Wales had huge EU-funding badges on everything. It told you what was going on, where your taxes were going. When Pembrokeshire voted to leave in 2016, they knew what they were doing. They understood the benefits, but still wanted out.

If you have the chance to go abroad, you'll see signs that say a project was funded by the council. In Mallorca I saw signs claiming responsibility for roadworks, playgrounds and other facilities. It was on bus maps. You knew when you were using something that the local council had paid for.

It's an easy step to take to try to make people more aware of the important role their local council plays, the decisions it has to make.

Spending decisions are so important for cash-strapped communities. What is worth prioritising? How many people need to use a library for it to be worth keeping open? Whatever your answer to that question, there are people who are going to disagree fiercely with you. If we put a number on how much each library cost the council, we could all have an opinion as to whether it was worth it.

That pothole? Yeah, we can fix that, but it'll cost the same as keeping a youth centre open for a day/month. If we reduced bin collections to once every three weeks rather than once a fortnight, there'd be plenty more money in the pot.

Once people become more aware of the types of decision being made, and the effects those decisions are having on their lives, they realise they have skin in that game. Come election time, they're ready and keen to vote.

There are a lot of different members of the council, though. You've probably got several versions of council or authority or assembly where you live. Keeping track of all of them is going to be a challenge.

We'll probably never get to the stage where we can have our *Where's the Councillor?* book. No beautifully drawn busy high streets, complete with libraries, but clear of potholes, with our local politicians waiting to be picked out of the crowds.

What we can do is make sure that people know what they're voting for, and what they're missing out on if they don't vote, even if they don't know exactly for whom they are casting their vote.

When they see that a library door is open and welcoming, or that the bins are being collected nicely or that a pothole has been filled in, they can look at it and think, 'I did that.'

X Factor

Celebrity-style political leadership

It all started with *Pop Idol*. In late 2001 and early 2002 at tea-time on Saturdays, up to 13 million people were wrapped up in a singing competition. We started with fifty singers, then got down to the final ten. Well, OK, it was the final nine because Rik Waller had to pull out (he was eventually replaced by Darius Danesh).

While there was a myriad of talents and personalities on show, it soon became clear that there were only two who had a chance of winning. Something about them, something more than their singing, had made them stand out from the crowd and captured the public's attention.

Will Young and Gareth Gates battled it out from mid December to early February. Each week they took a larger and larger share of the vote – on 12 January (ABBA week) they were up to 60 per cent of the vote between them. The four other singers couldn't get near them. Ironically Rosie Ribbons' losing song was 'The Winner Takes It All'.

After two seasons, *Pop Idol* was binned. Simon Cowell had a new, glitzier version. *The X Factor* took *Pop Idol* and turned up the volume. The contestants would now be mentored by celebrities. The all-knowing titans of the industry would style them, choose their songs, hone their image. They had to talk about their personal lives in press conferences. They had to sing solo, sing with their fellow contestants, sing off against each other to avoid crashing out.

What's good about *The X Factor* is that it's really clear what's going on. It's a competition to be a pop star. It's not just about the singing – hence all the lifestyle coaching and backstory drama. The person who the viewer thinks has that quality – the X factor – gets the most votes and wins.

Over the last few years, it really seems as if our politics has learned a lot from these shows as increasingly it all becomes about the personality of the leader. And one big personality can overshadow a lot of genuine talent elsewhere.

There has always been an element of showmanship in politics. A surprise (and pleasant) measure in the Budget is always known as a 'rabbit out the hat'. The Monster Raving Loony Party has been using election platforms as some kind of performance art for quite some time. In recent years it has been joined by many others, including Count Binface. But it never used to dominate the political landscape.

In the 1992 General Election, John Major famously took a soapbox around the country. He'd pitch up in the middle of your town, jump on his box so he could be seen and tell everyone why they should vote Conservative. He spoke to people; they spoke to him.

Fast forward thirty years and we live in a post-*X-Factor* world. There are hundreds of candidates, but we focus on the ones who are obviously going to win. The shift that has really changed politics is the slickness and the weaponised styling. Their clothes, their words, their hair, the locations in which they speak, everything is stage-managed by the possibly immortal titans of the industry.

The result is that everything is boiled down to sound-bite slogans: 'Get Brexit Done', 'Better off out', 'Strong and stable', 'Kinder, fairer politics', 'Stop the boats', even 'Hands, face, space'. Someone somewhere has decided that three is the magic number. It's enough to give the electorate a flavour of a message, without actually committing to anything. Like when you heard Shayne Ward doing a little bit of singing at Louis Walsh's bootcamp. The trouble with these slick soundbites is they take away from meaningful debate. We get caught up in showmanship, not detail.

It's not as if nobody saw this coming. In 1964 there was a suggestion that there would be TV debates for the General Election after Harold Wilson challenged Prime Minister

Alec Douglas-Home. The prime minister refused, saying, 'You'll get a sort of *Top of the Pops* contest. You'll then get the best actor as leader of the country and the actor will be prompted by a scriptwriter.'

Rightly or wrongly, though, this is the world in which we live. TV debates and the like are here to stay. Our only option is to take a close look and see what we can do with it.

Our first General Election TV debates came in 2010, between Gordon Brown, David Cameron and Nick Clegg. There were three televised events, one each on BBC, Sky and ITV. Millions tuned in (quite similar numbers to *The X Factor* at its heyday, in fact).

We had four and a half hours of debate, stretched across three weeks. It was compelling and it was useful. The electorate was engaged and the prospective prime ministers were (at least vaguely) interesting.

Simultaneously, the internet was heralding the end of election poster campaigns, as the photoshopped mocking versions were being widely spread before people had even seen the original. We were moving from standard advertising to full and open debate.

Despite everything, I'm a fan of this move. It's impossible to know how many of those millions of viewers watched the debates with an open mind, genuinely trying to choose who to vote for. I suspect that number is quite low. It's the opportunity, though, that you simply don't get with yet another attack billboard advert.

By 2015, we were really embracing the TV debate. We had four big ones. Anyone familiar with *The X Factor* will know about the format switch-up to make things interesting. We had Cameron v. Miliband. We had the leaders of seven different parties. We had the leaders of five parties, but without Cameron. We had Cameron, Miliband and Clegg. We even had nine separate single-issue debates with the candidates from seven different parties.

The BBC one was the most watched, pulling in nearly 9 million viewers. Nine million – and this was the one without the prime minister.

It was a truth universally acknowledged that an *X Factor* winner would have the Christmas Number One. And so it seemed with these debates. Surely, if you won those, you were guaranteed to be PM.

Real life is never so simple. The polls at the time suggested that Ed Miliband was a tiny bit ahead of David Cameron, who was only a tiny bit ahead of UKIP's Nigel Farage. David Cameron went on to win an unexpected majority.

Political campaigns carried on like this for a bit. There were big debates for the Brexit Referendum, including Nicola Sturgeon taking on Boris Johnson.

It was in 2017, though, that we really got a sense of what was to come. Theresa May debated Jeremy Corbyn a couple of times, but for the big BBC debate with all seven candidates, Amber Rudd was sent in May's place.

If you're not someone who comes across well on TV

– if you know you don't have the X factor – it doesn't suit you to try to take centre stage. Theresa May might have many qualities, but very few people thought that she had the X factor in person. The candidate who people did think had it was Jeremy Corbyn. That summer he would talk on the main stage at Glastonbury. That's a stage for people with the X factor.

In the end Corbyn came pretty close. We had a hung Parliament. May resigned.

Boris Johnson – a man who oozes X factor – entered the fray. This was a big turning point. Johnson had been knocking around for a long time, bringing his Number One hits wherever he went – as Mayor of London, on the Leave campaign. Everyone knew he was one day destined to become prime minister.

Johnson was happy to do the big debates – but refused to be grilled by Andrew Neil. That was important, because on the debate stage he could get away with all kinds of tricks, which he couldn't have done under the scrutiny of the famously difficult journalist.

Johnson would do TV – but only on his own terms. He wanted to be in control of his own narrative. At one point, when he was taken by surprise by a camera team at a dairy, he turned around and hid in an industrial fridge until they went away. He had ditched the framework of a voting show in favour of just doing his own thing. Like Harry Styles, but skipping the entire One Direction bit.

For him, reducing the debate to 'Get Brexit Done', saying that as frequently as he could on TV, on social media and wherever else, worked. Why allow himself to be scrutinised more?

Boris Johnson went on to win by miles and miles. He had so much more of the X factor than any other candidate, he drew millions of people to him. It helped that he was up against Jeremy Corbyn, whose own X factor appeared to have faded by this time. People disagree on the merits of Corbyn's policies, but what is clear is that in reality he is a details kinda guy, not a showman. Johnson used those debates to put the spotlight on himself and there was nothing anyone could do about it.

Since then, there has been talk about a bill that would require certain media commitments from party leaders at election time. It seems unlikely that this will happen any time soon, but Parliament does surprise us.

Maybe we could take it further, though. The viewing figures of these debates show there is an appetite for prime-time politics TV. *The X Factor* isn't on any more, but there are plenty of these shows that demonstrate a desire for slick event TV.

Let's embrace the whole thing. I want the House of Commons to go on tour. We know that PMQs is the big moment in the week, so let's take it round the country. Not just the big names. The whole House of Commons, using parliamentary rules that ensure everyone can get involved.

On Thursdays, the Commons has General Debates on current affairs. Imagine if an area of the country could vote on what the debates would be about. We'd then start at 5 p.m. in, say, the Manchester Arena. MPs could take part in a debate about topical and interesting things. Two ninety-minute debates, a time limit of three minutes per MP. MPs from that area would be given preference in terms of speaking.

Then, at 8 p.m., it would be PMQs. Live in front of 10,000 people, broadcast on BBC One.

We'd be giving regular, backbench MPs the opportunity to speak to the nation, to gain recognition from their constituents. We'd have the showbiz, the glamour of the prime minister taking questions from all-comers. We'd have firm guidelines to avoid a few individuals hogging the limelight, to ensure civility, to promote detail over reductive slogans.

It would be event TV, but also in-depth political debate. Everybody wins.

Y

Yardstick

How do we measure a government's record?

We are obsessed with progress and success. We set ourselves targets, have dreams, and we'll often step back to
consider how we're doing, what progress we're making.

Take sport. Every time you switch on the TV there are
new ways of measuring that success. How many passes a
player has made, the expected goals, the rotation speed, the
strike rate. I'm sure it's all very important, but we already
know exactly how to gauge the success of a sports team.

A successful sports team wins the league. On any given
weekend you can pick up a paper and look at the tables.
Whether it's cricket, rugby, football or netball, it's the position in the league that counts, not the latest result. It's there
in plain sight for you to assess the quality of the players, the

manager and the physiotherapists involved, based on how well the team has performed across the season.

It's clear, it's open and it's honest.

In some ways, that's true of the government. At election time, it makes a bunch of promises to the public. Then it has five years to get to work, to show us that it's making progress, to highlight its success stories. To convince us that we still want the same people running the joint. We need to decide if that is the case, if we're happy with their performance.

But whereas a team's position in the league is a clear demonstration of success or failure, it's way more complicated with the government's record. What yardstick are we supposed to use to measure success? There are so many different departments, so many variations in experience across the country, so many stories of success and failure, how should we judge overall progress? In short, how do we know if this government is any good?

One method that the media and politicians love is measuring through international comparisons. We're the best at such and such in the G7, we're the worst in Europe at something else.

These comparisons don't stand up to much scrutiny. We're very different from those other countries. All countries are very different from each other. We have different populations, different cultural values, different landscapes – both metaphorically and literally. We can't create a premier league of countries and look at how our results stack up. It's nonsense.

So we're left trying to judge the government's record on individual policies – and that is a very complicated web to untangle.

The Conservative Party manifesto in 2019 promised 'an Australian-style points-based system to control immigration'. Priti Patel introduced the system in 2021. You need a minimum of 70 points to apply. You get points for things like having a clear job offer (20) and speaking good English (10).

Is that a promise achieved, though? The system has been delivered in theory, but is the government in control of immigration? Net migration has gone up and up. How are we supposed to judge its performance on that commitment?

The more vague a manifesto pledge, the harder it is to pin it down. When a pledge of forty new hospitals is made, it's easy for us to imagine forty huge new buildings – like the main hospital in your area, I'm sure. It turned out, though, that many of these would be extensions or renovations to existing hospitals. What did the government mean by 'hospital'? If forty minor buildings are constructed, is that pledge met?

What about inflation? The government sets a target for inflation, but then events take over. The Bank of England is in charge of interest rates. How do we know what's the result of government choices and what's down to inevitable external factors out of their control? How are we supposed to judge its response to the latter?

How about taking into account the progress of time? We don't live in a vacuum. The world moves on. Things change. What was once a good idea might not be appropriate a few years later.

What even makes it a good idea in the first place? If a government delivers on something that had a certain amount of opposition, is that a success?

In the 1970s, Canary Wharf and the docklands area were falling apart, so Margaret Thatcher made an enterprise zone to encourage businesses to go there. Within fixed boundaries, there was a bit less tax and slightly looser regulations.

Now, forty years later, it is unquestionable that there is a lot going on. Canary Wharf is a very impressive area of London: our biggest skyscrapers, huge numbers of offices and shops and bars. You can even, should you wish, sit in a boat that's also a hot tub in a canal. If the aim was to have all of that, she did it.

Of course, if your definition of success is to not rip out a community that already exists, whose families had lived there for generations, you might consider this a failure.

We can see that, on this particular policy, the government absolutely did achieve what it set out to do. Its voters would be pleased. Not everyone else was, though. Many people still think of it as a move that has done permanent damage. Even a clear win might not feel like a success.

It's even harder now to measure success after the tumultuous years we've lived through.

The 2019 General Election was won by Boris Johnson on a three-word promise: 'Get Brexit Done.' He got a deal together, he got the votes in Parliament and we're now out of the EU. We have the power to control, change and modify any regulations that we'd like to control, change or modify.

Roughly four months after that General Election, the pandemic arrived at our shores. That changed everything. Of course it changed everything. Now we're constantly being told that we're living in unprecedented times. And we really do seem to be.

Hot on the heels of the virus, we've had war in Europe, inflation and the cost-of-living crisis. Naturally it's been a challenging time for the government, as well as for the rest of us. We need to take into account that a government can't always predict challenging times and natural disasters. Only a few scientists predicted a pandemic. Nobody could have included a policy of whether or not to send fighter jets to Ukraine in 2019. When something world-changing happens, the government has to react quickly to the new reality, sometimes coming up with new policies on the hoof. But how much slack should we cut it?

Measuring success during a time of national crisis is very difficult. Apart from the rule-breaking by Cummings, Hancock, Johnson, Sunak and more, did the government do a good job? The vaccine rollout was pretty special.

Was the furlough scheme a good idea? Did we need those lockdowns and should they have been longer or shorter, stricter or more relaxed? Would another party have done any better – or worse? We'll never get to compare a 'what if?' alternative reality.

We can look at some of the government's individual policies over that time. Let's take broadband. From 2019 to 2022 the percentage of people with access to gigabit broadband rose from 7 per cent to 70 per cent. At the same time, the target to get it out to everyone slipped from 2025 to 2030. What do we think? Is that a success story? That they managed to roll so much out during a pandemic is pretty impressive, right? But then again, adding a whole five years extra?

Perhaps we can look at an area we can all agree needs sorting: the number of people living in poverty in the UK. There is not a person in the country who wants people to be living in poverty. Might it be possible to use that as our yardstick?

Even that is tricky because there are different ways to measure poverty, and it can all get very complex. There was a PMQs once in which the leader of the opposition and the prime minister shouted at each other about poverty, both armed with statistics that apparently showed that the government was doing both terribly and an amazing job. Simultaneously.

Essentially there is absolute poverty – when people don't have enough money to cover their basic needs – and relative poverty, which is when people have 60 per cent less money than the median in the country.

The good news is that absolute poverty has been coming down for a long time. Since the 1990s we've seen fewer and fewer people in absolute poverty in the UK. This is good. And recently we've seen a drop in relative poverty – but that's because so many people now have less money, which means that the 60 per cent median line has dropped down. Officially, all of us having a little bit less than we used to brings other people out of poverty. That seems less good.

If these individual policies are impossible to evaluate clearly, if we can't find the questions with simple answers we'd all support, we need to find a different way.

Let's go back to the basics. What is the job of a government? It's to make the changes and run the country in the way that the public wants. So how well has the government done the things that people voted for it to do?

To really hold politicians to account for this, though, we need them to be much more specific at election time. Policies need to be front and centre of campaigns. Not just 'Get Brexit Done', but what exactly are you proposing for Brexit and how will it impact me?

In 2019, we were also told about creating 'more great schools', extra police officers and other bitesize digestible big-number policies. The detail was so vague, though. A big-book manifesto was published and if you took the time to read it, you'd be none the wiser on what exactly was supposed to be delivered by when.

These manifesto books need to have time frames on them. Schedules. Clarity. What will have happened by the end of year one? By the next Parliament. What can we expect to see in classrooms so we know they have created more great schools? When will those changes happen?

Then we could actually hold politicians to account on things without them being able to weasel their way out of it, by changing the definition of a 'new hospital' to include an extra wing. The personnel would matter less too. We would know fully well what we asked the government to do, so it can get rid of its PM a couple of times if it wants to – but then get back to the job of delivering on those promises. Fulfilling the contract with the voter.

It's now become customary for parties to publish their numbers in some kind of 'costings document'. They're there to show that there is real intent and promises are feasible. Very, very few people read these slightly confusing and technical documents. Journalists do, and challenge prospective candidates on them, but they're not a useful tool for the average member of the public.

A few years ago we were all being told to have SMART targets: specific, measurable, attainable, realistic and timely. It's clearly management nonsense, of course. I'm not quite sure of the difference between 'attainable' and 'realistic', but maybe you've got to make it spell SMART or it doesn't count. Whatever my personal reservations about the acronym, it's the right vibe. Measurable and timely.

Until then, we're stuck trying to judge each policy on its merit the best we can. Maybe we'll agree with the leader of the opposition more. Maybe with the prime minister. It's a lot for us to sift through and evaluate, but we really do need to know how good they are. We need to know where they are in the league. And if it might be time for new management.

Zero Emissions

When problems are too big for politics

My mother is a good egg. During my childhood, back in the late 1980s, she volunteered at a local museum, she gave blood regularly, she went to the library and selected classical records to play to people in what was then called an old people's home.

She also recycled her glass.

At that point in our country's journey to Net Zero, very few people recycled their glass. To do it we had to collect all our cola bottles, wine bottles and jam jars, pile them up in a corner of the house, then drive to the top level of the car park at the local Sainsbury's. Once there, each item had to be posted into the bottle bank one at a time. For some reason it was always raining when we went.

It must have been sunny occasionally, but memories are funny things.

That's a real commitment to recycling. A real commitment to reducing waste. And it's this sort of commitment that we need right now if we're to tackle one of the biggest issues we face today – one that politicians the world over are struggling to address.

The climate is changing. The world is getting hotter. The weather is becoming more extreme. We see forest fires and floods. We see habitats changing to the point where endangered animals end up homeless. We see the end scenes of every David Attenborough documentary when he shows us some miserable sights.

The people who are being most affected right now were already some of the most vulnerable in the world. Here in the UK, though, the impact isn't that bad yet. Apart from those Attenborough shows, we haven't really noticed it. Our climate has always been quite gentle, so the fact that 2022 was the hottest year ever in the UK (reaching an average temperature of over 10 degrees for the first time), or that all of the top ten hottest years since 1884 have taken place since 2003, doesn't feel too bad. We have warmer summers. If you don't think about it too much, it's almost desirable.

The real impact on our small island isn't going to get utterly horrific for quite some time. Our children will have it worse than us. Their children? Well, it's beginning to get pretty bad by then.

If watching the world burn from our slightly sunnier gardens and parks isn't motivating enough, if the fate of our future generations isn't motivating enough, it does create other problems for us here and now. The number of people displaced from their home countries by this stuff goes up every year. The more displaced people there are globally brings more refugees to our shores – and the refugee systems we've got in place aren't built to deal with this influx.

The more climate change affects other parts of the world, the more turbulence we see in those countries, including the rise of governments and leaders who aren't quite the cuddly and friendly ones we might want. The world is destabilised. Global politics becomes less safe.

It's bad for others now. It's bad for us now. It'll be worse for others in the future. It'll be worse for us in the future.

Which is why it matters that we take what action we can. Of course, we now know that recycling isn't the number one action that is going to save the environment – cutting out driving or flying, for example, has a greater effect – but it still has the potential to make a difference. The difficulties we find even with recycling, though, show just how hard it is to have an impact with even seemingly straightforward changes to our lives. The reality of the problem is so much greater than such a simple solution.

Recycling is great in theory. If I enjoy a cold can of something delicious, it's possible for that can to be completely reused afterwards. I could, in theory, drink another cold can of something delicious a few months later from exactly the same can, it having been scrunched down and remade. That's a whole can that doesn't need to be extracted from the ground in the mines of Venezuela.

These days recycling is also so much easier. Most of us have at least two bins. My council collects five different bins (although you do have to pay for the garden waste one these days). It's been a radical change – millions of households quietly getting on with sorting their rubbish so it can be recycled into something else. You no longer have to suffer the vagaries of the British weather to dispose of your empty Echo Falls bottles.

Once the council has picked it up, though, things get a bit more tricky. If your council recycles it in the UK, we know that it comes out all good and recycled. We can visit the site. It's all tracked. Perfect. Except it's super expensive to recycle everything in the UK.

For a local council, funds are incredibly, incredibly tight. It has to pay for a lot of things. Councillors might really want to send your rubbish to be processed in the UK, but they're definitely not going to cut social-care funding to make that happen, right? Maybe they are. That's a conversation they need to have in the town hall where they meet.

The other option is to send it off to be recycled elsewhere. The biggest sites in the world were all in China, but recently President Xi said he didn't want China to be a country where everyone sends their rubbish, so he stopped the industry overnight. Now there are lots of sites around the world, but global capacity has gone down.

The biggest problem with recycling your waste abroad is that once it's gone into those massive shipping containers, it's impossible to know if it really is, actually, 100 per cent recycled. The reality is that it probably isn't. Some of it will be sent to landfill, some of it will be burned. We can't know the percentage that is transformed into something new and usable.

This is just one decision-making process in the constant battle over our earth's finite resources. It's one where we know what we should do, but the realities mean we hardly ever do it. It's too expensive. Too inconvenient. We don't want to make the short-term sacrifices now to make a difference to a future we ourselves probably won't see.

There are a huge number of choices like this. A huge number.

We need to get people to use public transport not cars, which means investment in public transport. People like using their cars, though. Money is tight. We rumble on with small policies like capping bus tickets at £2. The number of people riding the bus goes up (which is good), but I'm not sure we've seen fewer cars on the road.

In London, Sadiq Khan started a new road charge for the most polluting cars. This is specifically a measure about air quality, but it's also good news for fans of zero emissions. Except in the outer areas especially, the public transport system isn't as extensive, so many people don't have the choice to ditch their cars. Also, who has the oldest, least efficient cars? People without much money. People who can't afford to buy new cars or to pay the extra charges.

We are currently looking for more fossil fuels in the North Sea. That's not something that is hugely popular with opposition MPs, who ask how we can possibly be looking for oil in 2023. The government says that we're moving towards a zero-emission future, but we're years away from that so it's better to have our own oil than depend on, say, Russia. It's about short-term security. The whole debate is incredibly bleak when both sides are making valid points.

The thing about global warming is that it's global. While there are now very few people who deny that climate change is happening or that human activity has contributed to it, there are plenty who will tell you that we can't do anything about it while India (for example) is pumping out even more emissions than we are. If it's hard to give up our cars and our whatever else, why go through this when it'll have minimal impact on a global scale? Placing aside arguments about the fairness of this for countries going through industrialisation many years later than the UK did, what we need is to find solutions that every nation will get behind.

We have climate-change world meetings every

few years. COP26 was held here in the UK. The Paris Agreement was made at one in, erm, Paris. All the Big Cheeses from around the world pitch up and – after a lot of work from people in suits behind the scenes – agree to reduce emissions together and make the world an idyllic, not-going-to-fry place.

They then go home and don't meet those targets. The time frame is extended, the targets slightly blurred.

The truth is that cutting emissions is hard. Managing to do so while maintaining our quality of life is harder. But the point is this. There is a train coming. We're on the tracks. At the moment, it feels as if it's quite far away, and we're quite comfortable on the tracks. It is coming, though. We need to find a way of dealing with it politically that's going to have a meaningful impact on that train.

Admittedly this isn't an easy thing to solve. No one has an answer. The tug-of-war over long-term climate policies versus what people need right now is real – and some of those short-term needs are valid.

Some politicians will say that technology will save us. Someone somewhere is going to come up with something that's going to make it all OK. We'll fund that tech if someone gets close. They'll make a tonne of money anyway, if it works. This is an excellent stance if you're a politician. It takes so much pressure off right now, if you can tell everyone we can just hold on until Silicon Valley or Imperial College saves us.

It is, of course, nonsense. We don't know that tech is coming. It's just a nice story to tell yourself when you go to bed after a 28°C summer afternoon by Loch Ness.

What we need is a political solution. We've committed to zero emissions; everyone agreed. We need to get on with it. To rally the people. To force corporations to play their part. We need to stop making lofty statements that don't line up with our actions. We need to stop waiting around for something to come to our rescue. Sometimes you've just got to stand up and be counted. We can't change what other countries do. We can only control what happens here. We can only lead by example. So let's do that.

We need politicians to work together across party lines. We need a new level of honesty with the people at election time. We need press briefings. We need data. We need referenda on decisions to get the public on board, to help us understand the tough decisions and long-term plans that have to be made. We need to learn to support actions that MPs take even if we don't agree with them, and be willing to accept a little more inconvenience in our lives when we can.

On this issue so many of the things we've discussed in this book come into play – long-term planning, consultation, debate, justification. Maybe if we can start making the small steps to improve our political landscape, it might just help us to work towards solving one of our biggest problems.

Conclusion

So there you have it. Twenty-six ways in which we can make politics better, more hopeful. Maybe even more productive.

Some of them are more achievable than others. I don't really expect to see PMQs at the Manchester Arena any time soon. I don't even expect it to be moved to prime-time TV.

I think that what every solution in here has in common is a desire for a more respectful and more caring political discourse. We're going to disagree on things. That's always going to happen. When it does, though, what are we going to do about it?

I read an excellent and articulate article by someone much cleverer than me about why we should never have another referendum. He was arguing about the paucity of information out there and the difficulty of people making informed decisions.

After reading his words, I went back to 'Referendum' in this book, more than a little scared about what I might have to change. I didn't change anything. I stand by it.

I think Tim Harford (whose article it was) makes a strong case, but I think that the opportunity for the country to have a grown-up discussion is too good to pass up.

That's the thing. When we're talking about making politics better, there is no one definitive answer. There certainly aren't twenty-six definitive answers. There will be things you didn't agree with in the book. That's OK. As long as it's not a preference for *Sing!* over *Jumanji*. I draw the line there.

At the start of the book, I said that we have to start somewhere. We have to change something, because the current state of affairs just isn't good enough. It might appear too big a task to tackle, but there are always things that can be done.

We could put big screens in Parliament Square so all visitors to the area can see what's going on, that it's a living, working building, not a museum.

We could have political shows based around daytime TV. There is a show in which experienced people go round helping others do up fancy houses in France. We could get two super politicians to visit a council that's trying to do something innovative and they could help them, show us the challenges and obstacles and how we might overcome them.

We could do *The Masked Singer*, but instead of singing they talk about their experiences of the NHS, and instead of being masked they're making earnest eye contact with the audience. OK, I've never watched *The Masked Singer*, maybe it's a bit of a departure from the format, but I still think this could work well.

I've barely even touched on electoral reform in all this. Would a proportional-representation system help? What about the campaign Votes at 16? Or even Votes at 11, when young people go to secondary school? What about mandatory voting? Voting online? Voting on a Saturday?

Maybe none of the above. Maybe you don't agree with any of it.

What I'm offering you, though, is a vision for the future. A future where politics isn't a dirty word, your voting intention doesn't mark you out as an enemy, where we're involved in the decisions that affect us, where just because we disagree with someone doesn't mean we have to resort to hate and aggression.

I'm offering some long-term ideas that take into account the paths people want to tread. One that prioritises kindness, understanding and hope.

Lovely reader, come with me. Let's see what we can do together.

Acknowledgements

Every time I was struggling with this book, the Wonderful Katie would step in and help. She gave me ideas, she gave me space, she gave me love. The A–Z format of this was her idea. Thank you, Katie.

When I needed a bit of enthusiastic cheerleading, I could always turn to my beautiful children: Elliot, Caitlin, Alfred and Felix. They've got my back and I love them, even if they sometimes eat with their mouths open.

None of this would have been possible without the amazing people in the SP family. That's Diane and Charlotte of Team SP, but also everyone we've ever interacted with in person or online. Simple Politics has been my life for years and years. You did this. Thank you, x.

Finally, my own Instagram community. I write about mental health and other things on there, and we have just the most incredible group of people. Supportive, caring, interested and interesting. You mean more to me than you could know.

ABOUT THE AUTHOR

Tatton Spiller is the author of *The Breakdown* and the founder of Simple Politics. SP has been helping people engage with politics for the best part of a decade, gaining over a million social media followers in the process. When things are complex in politics, people turn to him and his team. Individually, Tatton talks to as many people as possible about politics, on TV and radio (including BBC Two, Sky News and 5Live), with live audiences, in schools, on podcasts and more. With a background in classroom teaching, journalism, education at the Houses of Parliament and event production, nobody writes about politics in the way he does.